IMAGES OF W

T–54/55
THE SOVIET ARMY'S
COLD WAR MAIN
BATTLE TANK

Polish-built T-55s on exercise.

IMAGES OF WAR

T–54/55
THE SOVIET ARMY'S
COLD WAR MAIN
BATTLE TANK

RARE PHOTOGRAPHS FROM
WARTIME ARCHIVES

Anthony Tucker-Jones

Pen & Sword
MILITARY

First published in Great Britain in 2017 by
PEN & SWORD MILITARY
an imprint of
Pen & Sword Books Ltd,
47 Church Street,
Barnsley,
South Yorkshire
S70 2AS

Every effort has been made to trace the copyright of all the photographs.
If there are unintentional omissions, please contact the publisher in writing, who
will correct all subsequent editions.

A CIP record for this book is available from the British Library.

ISBN 978 1 47389 109 8

Typeset by CHIC GRAPHICS

Printed and bound by CPI Group (UK) Ltd, Croydon, CR0 4YY

Pen & Sword Books Ltd incorporates the imprints of Pen & Sword Archaeology,
Atlas, Aviation, Battleground, Discovery, Family History, History, Maritime, Military,
Naval, Politics, Railways, Select, Social History, Transport, True Crime, Claymore
Press, Frontline Books, Leo Cooper, Praetorian Press, Remember When, Seaforth
Publishing and Wharncliffe.

For a complete list of Pen & Sword titles please contact
Pen & Sword Books Limited
47 Church Street, Barnsley, South Yorkshire, S70 2AS, England
E-mail: enquiries@pen-and-sword.co.uk
Website: www.pen-and-sword.co.uk

Contents

Introduction:
First All-Rounder

There can be no understating the significant role played by the T-54/55 tank in the Cold War and in the decade following it. While the Kalashnikov AK-47 became the people's gun, the T-54/55 became the people's tank. The T-54 and its variants was the most prolific tank ever produced and the very first dedicated Soviet main battle tank as opposed to light, medium or heavy – it was the first all-rounder. It proved to be a very worthy successor to the famous T-34, which helped the Red Army gain victory during the Second World War.

The T-54/55 was easily the most successful tank of the Cold War and was involved in almost every single major conflict since the 1950s from Budapest to Baghdad. In fact, the T-54 series has seen more action than any other post-Second World War tank. Although it was rapidly outdated, the T-54/55 formed the backbone of the Warsaw Pact's tank forces and was widely exported around the world, seeing combat with numerous armies well into the early 2000s.

Remarkably, the T-54 was so popular that it even outlasted its successor the T-62. It remained in production for over thirty years, until 1981, by which time worldwide well over 70,000 had been built, easily outstripping the T-34 and making it the most ubiquitous tank of all time. In contrast only 20,000 T-62s had been built when production ended six years earlier in 1975. One of the reasons for this was that the T-62 cost up to three times as much to produce and the only real advantage it could offer was its heavier gun. All its other capabilities were broadly comparable.

While Moscow never released any official figures for T-54/55 production, it has been estimated that the Soviet Union alone built about 50,000. It was also manufactured in China, Czechoslovakia, Poland and Romania with approximately another 27,000 bringing total numbers to around 77,000. Some sources even put the total global figure as high as 100,000. This beats T-34 numbers hands down, even allowing for post-war T-34 construction by Czechoslovakia and Poland, amounting to about 60,000. This makes the T-54/55 the most widely-used tank in history – a quite remarkable achievement.

Despite its incredible track record, the T-54/55 remains overshadowed by almost every other Cold War tank. Indeed, the Soviet T-62 and T-72 achieved far greater notoriety during the numerous regional conflicts of the Cold War and the subsequent wars after the collapse of the Soviet Union.

Photograph Sources

All photographs are via the author. The publishers and the author are particularly indebted to Tim and Preston Isaac, the proprietors of the Cobbaton Combat Collection, for generously making their Czech-built T-54 available for a detailed photo shoot. The author is also grateful to Dan Reoch of D&B Militaria for supplying samples of inert former Warsaw Pact T-54/55 tank rounds and training rounds.

Photos of preserved Chinese tanks in the Beijing Military Museum were taken by Max Smith. Graham Thompson also ably assisted with photos of the Polish-built version. Max Smith and Gerry van Tonder provided shots of the Czech armoured recovery version. Vasco Barbic kindly offered guidance on the Egyptian tanks. This book would be much poorer without their assistance and expertise. Any errors though are solely the author's

Chapter One

Heir Apparent – T-54

Towards the end of the Second World War the Soviets decided that rather than maintaining large fleets of dedicated light, medium and heavy tanks they needed a good all-rounder – this resulted in the main battle tank (MBT) concept. A 'one size fits all' solution.

Soviet tank designers began to look at developing a successor for the T-34/85 medium tank and the IS (Ioseph Stalin) heavy tank. Drawing on their experiences with the T-34/76, T-34/85, KV-85 and IS-1/2, in 1944 they came up with the T-44, which bore a striking resemblance to the late-war T-34/85 and was armed with the same 85mm gun.

It was essentially the same tank with a number of modifications. The main improvements to the rugged T-34/85 design were a similar-shaped turret but without the characteristic thick turret neck, plus a better-shaped hull. Other improvements included a transverse-mounted engine and transmission and torsion-bar suspension. The crew was reduced from five in the T-34/85 to four in the T-44.

T-44 Medium Tank

One of the designers' tasks was to lower the height of the T-34/85 that first went into service in the summer of 1944. Upgunning the T-34/76 had resulted in a much bigger turret, which increased the T-34's height from around 2.4m to over 2.7m. While the improvement from 76.2mm gun to 85mm gun was very welcome, it made the T-34/85's bulky turret a much better target. Similarly, the IS heavy tank was almost 3m high.

On the T-44 one way to achieve a lower silhouette was to eliminate the prominent collar at the turret base. The hull side armour, which on the T-34 was sloped, was vertical and thicker. This was to permit a wider turret ring because the turret's armour was more slanted than that on the T-34/85. Another way that the height was reduced was by installing the diesel engine transversely. Also the Christie spring suspension was replaced with a torsion-bar suspension. The result was that the T-44 had a height of just under 2.5m.

Improving on the T-34/85's main armament was unsuccessful. Attempts were made to upgun the T-44 with a 122mm tank gun but the turret was too small, although experiments with a 100mm gun were slightly more promising. However, only a few prototypes were ever built and the production T-44 retained the 85mm gun. The only way to get round this problem was to design a new tank with a larger turret.

While the T-44 was very similar to the T-34, the glacis plate at the front was much steeper which meant it had to be thicker. The driver was only provided with a very narrow vision slit in the glacis and his hatch, located next to the hull machine gun on the glacis on the T-34, was repositioned to the hull roof. The hull gunner was dispensed with in line with the existing trend with Soviet heavy tanks. Protection against infantry was provided by a Degtyarev 7.62mm machine gun mounted in a fixed position next to the driver, which was fired through an opening in the glacis plate. This was a feature later retained in the T-54.

The successful T-34 five road-wheel running gear was largely unchanged, although the T-44 had a wider gap between the first and second pairs of road wheels instead of the second and third as on the T-34. One of the drawbacks of the latter was that it employed the American Christie-style suspension. This meant that bulky springs took up a large amount of space inside the tank. Efforts to remedy this with the T-34M in 1941 had to be abandoned because of the outbreak of war. The T-43 partially remedied this but was swiftly superseded by the need for a larger gun and the T-34/85 which used the existing T-34 hull.

The T-44 proved problematic especially where its weight was concerned. It was supposed to be the same as the T-34/85 at some 31.5 tons, but in light of the thicker armour and lengthening of the hull, it is hard to see what the lowering of the height achieved other than to reduce the tank's silhouette. It is suspected that the T-44 was heavier than its predecessor and suffered from problems with its running gear and transmission.

In the event only a few thousand T-44s were ever built at Kharkov and it did not see much, if any, combat at the end of the war. It was allegedly deployed briefly during the Hungarian uprising of 1956. After proving unreliable in front-line service the tank was rebuilt as the T-44M and continued to be used into the 1970s – largely in a tank driver training role. From the design faults and teething problems it is evident that the T-44 was very much an interim design and testbed for features that were incorporated in the vastly more successful T-54.

T-54 Main Battle Tank

The key lesson that the Red Army learned from the Second World War was that you needed a lot of everything, especially tanks, to wage modern armoured and mechanized warfare. It was clear from the T-34 and T-44 that they required a tank that was easy to mass-produce in vast numbers, was very reliable and armed with at least a 100mm gun. While the IS heavy tank had been armed with a massive 122mm gun, it meant that it was 20 tons heavier than the T-34/85. Experience showed that there was no long-term future in heavy tanks. Thus was born the T-54 MBT.

The T-54 was effectively a Ukrainian tank. Under the designation of Obiekt 137 (or B-40) it was designed by the Morozov Bureau at the Malyshev Plant in Kharkov, Ukraine. The city had been producing T-34s at the start of the Second World War but was captured during the German invasion. It subsequently became the scene of a series of battles fought between the Wehrmacht and the Red Army before being finally liberated. However, the Kartsev Bureau at Nizhnyi Tagil in Russia would take the credit for the T-54/55.

The T-54 made its debut in the late 1940s with the first prototype appearing in 1946 and initial production authorized three years later. Three factories were given the task, at Kharkov, Nizhnyi Tagil and Omsk. It and the subsequent T-55 went through numerous upgrades, rebuilds and reconfigurations and unless you are a specialist technical intelligence expert trying to identify them all is a largely fruitless task (some sources are downright contradictory or are simply incorrect). Essentially the T-54 and T-55 were the same tank with detailed improvements. The following lists the key T-54 production models.

T-54-1 (Model 1946)

This bore some resemblance to the T-44, with undercuts to the front and rear of the turret. Similarly, it also had a very wide gun mantlet but was armed with the 100mm D-10T tank gun. These features made the turret vulnerable to enemy fire. It was issued to field units for trials but proved unsatisfactory and in the meantime the focus remained on T-34/85 production.

T-54-2 (Model 1949)

This was the very first low-rate production model with an improved turret that eliminated the frontal undercut, featured an overhang at the rear and was armed with the 100mm D-10T tank gun.

T-54-3 (Model 1951)

Second low-rate production model, featuring a turret undercut at the rear and a narrow, so-called 'pig snout' gun mantlet.

T-54 (Model 1953)
First full-rate production T-54 with a hemispherical turret with no rear undercut and narrow mantlet. This turret became standard on all subsequent models of the T-54/55.

T-54A (Model 1955)
This version was fitted with a fume extractor just behind the muzzle and vertical axis stabilization for the newer 100mm D-10TG gun, as well as power elevation. It was the first T-54 to have OPVT river-fording equipment, that enabled the tank to wade through water up to 5m deep and up to 700m wide. Other improvements included an electric oil pump, bilge pump, modified air filter and automatic fire-extinguisher system. Some Model 1955 retrospectively had infra-red might vision equipment installed. It was also produced by Czechoslovakia, Poland and China with some modification. Confusingly it is also known as the T-54A Model 1951.

T-54B (Model 1957)
The Model 1957 was a Model 1955 with improvements to its main armament and night-vision equipment for the commander, driver and gunner. This comprised an improved 100mm D-10T2S gun with an L-2 infra-red searchlight mounted next to the barrel. The gunner's standard MK-4 periscope was upgraded by the TPN-1 night observation device. The commander was served by a smaller searchlight known as the OU-3. This type of tank was also sometimes called the T-54B Model 1952.

T-54M (Model 1983/1988)
This upgraded the T-54A/B to T-55M standard with additional armour, the inclusion of an upgraded suspension, new tracks and interior improvements including a new engine and radio. This model was developed as the Obeikt 140. It set the benchmark for the last of the Cold War T-54/55s.

T-10: Last of the Heavies
Despite the rise of the main battle tank, the Soviet Union persisted with heavy tanks for a number of years after the end of the Second World War. The innovative IS-3, armed with a 122mm gun, appeared in the closing months of the war and was retained in service until the 1960s, though despite modifications it remained unreliable. It was followed by the short-lived IS-4 which needed redesigning.

Just after the T-54 went into full production, in 1956 the Soviets produced the largely forgotten T-10 Lenin heavy tank (or IS-10) armed with a 122mm gun. This looked very similar to the IS-3 and likewise had a round 'mushroom-head' turret giving the tank a low silhouette. It featured seven road wheels either side and three return rollers, whereas the IS-3 had six and three. This was presumably in an attempt to address some of the power-to-weight problems experienced by the latter tank. The IS engine and gearbox had simply not been up to the job.

Ironically, although classed as a heavy the T-10 was in fact lighter than the later American Abrams, British Chieftain and German Leopard. It proved to be the very last of the Soviet heavy tanks for good reason. The T-10 was flawed and by the 1960s did not meet the Soviet Army's developing all-arms tank doctrine. Despite armour of up to 270mm, its slow speed, limited ammunition stowage, low rate of fire and poor depression on the main gun greatly reduced its combat effectiveness. In particular, it meant that the T-54 had to slow down to allow the cumbersome T-10 to keep up. The IS tanks suffered the same problem in supporting the T-34 in 1945. The T-10 at 51 tons was 15 tons heavier than the T-54 and could manage at best 42km/hr compared to the T-54's 48km/hr.

The T-10 first appeared publicly in the November 1957 Moscow parade, but it was not long before it was relegated to a tank destroyer role. It was evident it could function as a long-range anti-tank support weapon, but as a spearhead tank it was just too slow. In addition, its thick armour might have made it suitable for local counter-attacks, but little else.

Although possibly deployed in Warsaw Pact countries by the Soviet Army, the T-10 was never exported and did not see combat during the Cold War. Some sources suggest it was supplied to Egypt and Syria but there is no evidence to support this and they are probably confusing it with IS-3M exported to Egypt in the 1960s and employed in the Six Day War. It is possible that some IS-4 and T-10 were shipped to Egypt for evaluation by the Soviet advisory teams but never handed over, though this would have been pointless as the Soviets were phasing out their heavy tanks.

Although ultimately a dead end, the heavy tank legacy should not be underestimated. Soviet post-war heavy tank production amounted to about 9,000, of which around 1,000 were IS-3M/IS-4 and the rest were T-10 and T-10M. However, by this stage Soviet doctrine and tank design was firmly focused on the main battle tank as the key armoured vehicle of the Soviet Army. The T-54 remained firmly the heir apparent.

Before the Second World War ended the Soviets decided to produce a successor to the war-winning T-34/85 medium tank – the T-54 MBT proved to be its heir.

The interim T-44 was little more than a basic reworking of the T-34/85. The new hull shape was the most significant change and the driver's hatch was replaced by a crude vision slit in the glacis plate. The rubber-rimmed spoked spider wheels used on the T-34 were retained.

Note the difference in the turret collar on the T-44 compared to the T-34/85 on the right. This was done in an attempt to reduce the overall height of the tank.

Looking similar to the T-44 but with a redesigned turret and bigger gun is the T-54-1 which appeared in 1946. The undercuts around the turret and the wide mantlet made it vulnerable: in particular the former created shot traps. This example has been upgraded at some stage as it has the later starfish-style wheels.

This preserved T-54-1 retains the original spider wheels.

T-54-2 under construction – this had a new turret design that reduced the undercuts to just the rear, plus introduced a narrow 'pig snout' gun mantlet.

A column of T-54-2s on manoeuvres – the third version of the turret would dispense with the shot trap at the back.

Early T-54 without the fume extractor, which was introduced on the T-54A, or the barrel counterweight. Note the shape of the coaxial machine gun opening and the gunner's sight aperture (left to right), either side of the 100mm gun. On the Czech and Polish-built versions the gunner's aperture is a different shape.

The T-54 Model 1953 introduced a hemispherical turret with no undercuts that became standard on all subsequent T-54/55 models. The twin handrails either side of the turret made their debut with the T-54-1 and were a result of the Soviet Army's paucity of armoured personnel carriers which meant supporting infantry had to hitch a ride.

Early T-54 with the spider wheels. It is also fitted with infra-red searchlights introduced with the T-54B, but no laser rangefinder.

The T-54A or Model 1955 was the second full-rate production model and featured a distinctive fume extractor. It was also built by China, Czechoslovakia and Poland. This preserved example belonged to the Polish Army.

The Ioseph Stalin heavy tank, in this case a later IS-7 developed in 1948, was a hangover from the Second World War. The T-54 MBT was designed to dispense with the need for light, medium and heavy tanks.

The Soviets built one last heavy tank in 1956 called the T-10 to support the T-54 but it was too slow and could not keep up with it.

Two views of the anti-aircraft machine-gun mount fitted to the loader's hatch for the 12.7mm DShKM on both the T-54 and T-55. The two long objects just beneath the weapon are equilibrator tubes needed to balance it.

Chapter Two

Up Close and Personal

Whilst the T-54's five road wheels either side of the hull and the rear drive sprocket and front idler are similar to those on the T-34, the round turret and 100mm gun are completely different. Nonetheless, the influence of the T-34 and T-44 is very evident.

Turret

The most obvious difference between the T-34 and T-54 is the latter's hemispherical or 'mushroom-dome' turret, that was installed on the T-54 Model 1953 onwards. This shape may have been influenced by the innovative round 'frying pan' turret designed for the late-war IS-3 heavy tank, which provided excellent shot-deflection surfaces. The IS-1 and IS-2 had turrets that were similar to the T-34/85.

The T-54 turret is made from a single casting with a roof plate made of two D-shaped pieces of armour welded on and fitted with two hatches. This design affords good ballistic protection and importantly including the cupola ensured that the tank is only 2.4m high, making it 0.3m lower than the T-34/85 and fractionally lower than the troubled T-44.

The second production T-54 Model 1951 initially had an oval-shaped turret with a small cutaway at the rear where it met the hull. This was dispensed with as it created a potential shot trap. A distinctive ventilator done is on the top right side of the turret and tank-rider handrails are welded to both sides of the turret. The T-54 and T-55 turret have 203mm of armour at the front and 150mm at the sides.

While the low turret offers a small target for enemy tanks, this was only achieved by jamming three of the crew into an extremely small space. In comparison the fighting compartment in the T-34/85 is positively roomy. Inside the T-54 turret the commander and gunner are squeezed together seated to the left of the 100mm gun, one behind the other with the loader seated to the right opposite the coaxial 7.62mm machine gun. All three had to ensure they were seated when in action because the T-54 and early T-55s had no rotating turret floor. This meant if they were standing during rotation they would be crushed by the gun breech. Only three rounds can be stored in the turret, which means once expended the loader has to leave his seat to get the shells stored in the floor storage racks.

Both the commander and gunner can operate the turret power control, which is electrohydraulic with manual controls for emergencies. The traverse rate is 360 degrees in 21 seconds. The commander has a cupola with a single-piece forward-opening hatch. In combat the commander constantly rotates the cupola searching for targets.

Forward of the commander's cupola is a periscope served by a TPK-1 sight, which gives the commander visibility up to 400m at night. On locating a target the commander rotates the turret. The gunner, with a TSH 2-22 sight that functions out to 800m, then engages. The loader has a periscope and single-piece hatch that opens rearwards. The Soviets later enhanced the primitive fire-control system with the addition of a laser rangefinder, which greatly increased the effectiveness of the 100mm gun.

D-10 Tank Gun

The D-10 series of rifled tank guns were originally designed utilizing a 100m naval round. The Model 1944 high-velocity gun first went into action in the summer of 1944 when it was used to arm the SU-100 tank destroyer. This derivative of the T-34 proved highly effective though the length of the barrel was inhibiting. The first tank gun version, known as the D-10T, was installed on a number of testbed vehicles before being used to arm the early-model T-54.

The subsequent version, drawing on previous improvements, was the D-10TG with a bore evacuator and stabilization in the vertical plane. This was followed by the D-10T2S with stabilization in both the horizontal and vertical planes. The latter has a muzzle velocity of 900 metres a second. The maximum range for direct fire is 6,000m and 15,000m for indirect fire, though is only really effective at a fraction of these ranges. The gun can manage a rate of fire of seven rounds a minute.

All these guns fired the same fixed ammunition. The recoil system comprises a hydraulic buffer and a hydropneumatic recuperator. They had horizontal sliding wedge breech blocks but none of them were fitted with muzzle brakes. In the T-54/55 the gun took 15–20 seconds to reload because the gun had to be fully elevated to enable the loader to extract the empty casing and load a fresh round.

The 100mm gun for the T-54 was built at the Artillery Plant No. 9 ordnance factory. This facility was set up in 1942 during the Second World War to develop and build towed artillery, anti-tank guns and howitzers as well as guns for tanks and self-propelled guns. These included the 100mm D-10T for the T-54, the D-10TG for the T-54A and the D-10T2S for the T-54B, T-54C and T-55 and T-55A. It not only produced the guns for the T-54/55 but also for the T-62, T-64, T-72, T-80 and the T-90.

Hull

Welded rolled plate was used to fabricate the T-54's hull, the sides of which are vertical except in the middle where a small overhang allows for the turret ring. Along the track guards either side are stowage bins, plus fuel and oil tanks. Likewise, at the rear of the hull brackets are fitted to permit the attachment of additional fuel tanks and smoke cylinders

To strengthen the nose, the glacis plates were designed with locking joints. A distinctive splash guard was installed across the glacis midway up. The glacis offers 97mm of protection at 58 degrees on the upper surface and 99mm at 55 degrees on the lower surface. The hull sides are protected by 79mm of armour. The hull roof to the rear grants access to the cover plates over the engine and the cooling grilles.

Driver's Compartment

As in the T-34 the driver's position is on the left, but the small driver's hatch is located on the hull roof rather than the glacis plate. Like the T-54's fighting compartment, the driver position is much more cramped than in the T-34. It is equipped with the normal tank controls, although the left and right steering levers have additional functions. The steering levers and foot controls are placed conventionally, with the gear-change lever on the far right. Two periscopes are below and forward of the driver's hatch cover. The double-clutching to change gear and the suspension system make the T-54/55 an exhausting drive, particularly under combat conditions. The bow 7.62mm machine gun is mounted just to the right of the driver and is fired by the driver using a button on the right steering lever.

Suspension

The suspension on the T-54 is the torsion bar variety, with five large road wheels each side, which have a characteristic gap between the first and second. They are double rimmed with rubber tyres and fitted to transverse torsion bars with hydraulic shock absorbers on the first and fifth wheels. The drive sprocket is at the rear and the idler at the front. The track shoes or links are held together in the same way as the T-34, using dry pins whose heads are on the inner edge of the tracks and are driven back into position by a raised surface on the final drive housing.

Engine

The engine is largely the same as that in the T-34. However, the increased width of the T-54 meant it could be installed transversely, as in the T-44, making more economical use of the space. Designated the V-54 engine it is a V-12 water-cooled diesel giving 520hp and 2,000rpm. The transmission is manual with five forward gears and one reverse. The coolant radiator and oil cooler are situated horizontally over the gearbox. The latter is manually operated and constant mesh in design with six gears (five forward and one reverse) with synchromesh on the top three forward.

Two steering boxes are fitted either side of the gearbox and are double stage planetary, with single epicyclic gear train and interlocking clutch between planet carrier and sun pinion. This permits the system to be used as the main braking unit, auxiliary gearbox and for steering. The driver's steering brakes have three positions. Once fully forward the interlocking clutches engage, then the sun pinions and planet carrier rotate as one, the steering and main brakes are disengaged and the drive is direct from the gearbox to the final reduction gears.

Pulled back into first position a single lever will disengage the appropriate clutch and the tank will turn on a single radius. When two levers are applied a reduction of 1.42:1 is gained between the input and output shafts on the steering box. This allows an increase in traction without using the main gearbox and can be used over broken ground. Pulling a single lever to the second position engages the main brake on that side though both clutch and steering brakes are disengaged, which causes a skid turn in the desired direction. If both are pulled back or the foot brake is used the main brakes halt the tank. If the steering levers are left in this position they act as parking brakes.

Torque from the crankshaft is first passed through a reduction unit. This turns the drive through 180 degrees and reduces the speed by 0.7:1. The clutch is of the mutliplate, steel on steel variety and is attached to the gearbox casing. Drive to the cooling fan is provided at this point as well via another friction clutch that avoids damaging the fan during abrupt engine speed changes.

As in the T-34 the engine in the T-54 is started electrically, and again as with the T-34, in very cold weather or if the battery is flat a secondary compressed-air system can be used to turn over the engine. The T-55 is equipped with an AK-150 air compressor that refills the air pressure cylinders. This means it uses a compressed-air engine start up with the electrical starter as a back-up.

There is a two-stage air filtration: the first employs a centrifugal cleaner, kept clean by back pressure from the exhaust; the second employs oil-wetted elements. Lubrication is of the conventional sump type, including a heater coil for cold weather. Likewise, a heating element is also in the pressurized cooling system. Exhaust gases are expelled through a rectangular cowling on the left track guard.

Opposite above and below: The T-54/55 has a distinct gap between the first and second road wheels. On the right-hand side above the track guards there are three external armoured fuel tanks. On the left are three to four stowage bins for tools and the exhaust outlet.

The narrow vertical plate running horizontally across the glacis is designed to stop water rushing up the front when fording shallow rivers and inundating the driver. The tiny hole just below it is the opening for the bow machine gun. The prominent mounting lugs welded to the lower nose plate are for attaching a dozer blade.

This shot shows the three external armoured fuel tanks fitted on the right-hand side of the tank, as well as the rear-mounted external 200-litre fuel drums. On the Polish version of the T-54A additional fuel cells were also positioned either side of the turret ring.

Close-up of the main armament mantlet NBC/rain cover and the coaxial machine gun opening cover.

The 100mm D-10T gun fume extractor which is set back from the muzzle.

Muzzle showing the barrel rifling.

The commander's and the loader's hatches open in opposite directions. The commander's hatch on the left shows the cupola optics as well as the commander's sight.

Bolted-on mounting for the commander's cupola and gunner's left-hand turret periscope. From the T-54B onwards the tank was equipped with the Luna night-fighting system. As part of this the gunner's MK-4 periscope was replaced with the TPN-1 night observation device.

T-54 turret ventilator dome with rain cover, forward and to the left of the loader's hatch, and the loader's right-hand MK-4 turret periscope. The dome was omitted on the T-55 and is the easiest way to tell the two apart.

Driver's single-piece access hatch and twin periscopes.

Driver's periscopes. One of these can be substituted for an infra-red periscope to be used with the infra-red light mounted on the right side of the glacis plate.

Headlights mounted in a protective frame on the right side of the glacis: one is restricted white light, the other infra-red.

Rear engine deck showing the rectangular fan and rounded engine grills.

T-54 rear drive sprocket.

Typical cast double road wheel. These are the later starfish design that replaced the T-34-style spider wheels.

Front idler.

Twin road wheel showing how the track shoes engage.

The T-54/55 track shoes are held together by dry pins.

The extremely cramped driver's position with the hatch open.

Driver's pedals comprising, left to right, clutch, brake and accelerator. The steering levers are positioned either side.

Coaxial machine gun to the right of the main gun.

Gunner's telescopic sight to the left of the 100mm gun plus the traverse and elevation controls.

The automatically-operated bow machine gun situated just to the right of the driver. This fires through a small hole in the glacis plate.

Chapter Three

Fine Tuning – T-55

The subsequent T-55, under the designation Obiekt 155, was not developed by the Morozov Bureau in Ukraine, but by the Kartsev Bureau at Nizhnyi Tagil in Russia. It went on to design the T-62 and the subsequent T-72 and T-90 MBTs. By this stage, Morozov was concentrating its efforts on the flawed T-64 prototypes. The basic design changes that resulted in the T-55 were with the engine, transmission and gun stabilization. Essentially, therefore, the T-54 and T-55 were one and the same beast, but built at different locations.

The power plant for the T-55 was an improved model twelve-cylinder V-55 water-cooled diesel engine, generating 580hp, which was 60hp more than the earlier V-54 in the T-54. This resulted in a slightly improved performance and power-to-weight ratio. The transmission was improved accordingly and the fuel capacity boosted to offer a 25 per cent increase in radius of operation. Total fuel capacity in the T-54 was 812 litres, increased to 960 litres in the T-55.

The T-55's turret was changed slightly from the basic T-54 design, which had cupolas for both the commander and the loader plus the circular mushroom ventilator dome near the front of the roof. Some late T-54s only had the commander's cupola, as did the T-55, though in its case the tell-tale ventilator was also omitted. Therefore the easiest way to distinguish the T-55 from the T-54 is by the absence of the dome and the loader's cupola.

Like the T-54 before it, the T-55 was armed with a 100mm gun, with a coaxial machine gun and another fixed machine gun in the front of the hull. The latter though is omitted from later models of the T-55. The T-54, apart from the earlier models, had the 100mm gun stabilized in elevation and depression only, while in contrast the T-55 was provided with stabilization in both the vertical and horizontal planes, improving accuracy while on the move.

The following lists the key T-55 production models.

T-55 (Model 1958)

This was essentially a T-54 with a new turret without the rooftop mushroom ventilator dome. It also had a more powerful V-55 diesel engine. The ammunition load was increased to forty-three rounds and the turret had a new stabilizer. Like the later models of T-54, it was armed with the D-10T2S gun.

T-55A (Model 1961)

As the Cold War escalated and the threat posed by nuclear, biological and chemical (NBC) weapons became ever more serious it was decided to provide the T-55 with radiation shielding. This included a NBC system with improved fire detection and suppression. Other improvements consisted of an air compressor for starting, redesigned front fuel tanks and ammunition stowage. The deep-water fording capability was improved, as were the tank's shock absorbers.

Additional changes were made to the close-defence weapons. The earlier 7.65mm SGMT machine guns were replaced by a single 7.62mm PKT. The fixed bow machine gun was dispensed with to permit another six rounds of 100mm ammunition to be carried. The exhaust outlet was modified to allow it to lay a smoke screen. The crew were also provided with night vision equipment.

T-55 (Model 1970)

This was simply a T-55A with the mount for a 12.7mm anti-aircraft gun fitted over the loader's hatch which was fitted to the T-62. The same conversion was carried out to the T-55 (Model 1958) to create the T-55A (Model 1970).

T-55M (Model 1983/1988)

By the 1970s the T-54/55 needed modernizing if its service life was to be extended. This was achieved by enhancing its armament and armour resulting in the T-55M. It was upgraded with the 9K116 Bastion laser beam-riding missile system, fired from the 100mm gun, plus passive armour protection, a V-55U engine and R-173 radio system. Bastion used the 3UBK-10 round with the 9M117 missile (NATO designation AT-10 'Stabber'): the round propelled the missile out of the gun barrel and then the sustainer motor cut in. All the operator had to do was keep the target designated. Bastion had a range of 4,000m.

The additional armour, comprising layers of armour plate with space between filled with penopolyurethane, was fitted either side of the turret and on the glacis plate. On the sides 10mm armoured skirts formed of steel reinforced rubber sections were added to give the hull extra protection. The belly of the tank under the driver was also up-armoured.

T-55M-1 (Model 1983/1988)

As above but with the V-46-5M engine used in the T-62. Those tanks fitted with this engine were given the -1 designator.

T-55MV (Model 1983/1988)

T-55M fitted with Kontakt explosive reactive armour (ERA) – with the V short for *vzyvnoi* or explosive. This development was in response to Israel's Blazer ERA used in Lebanon in 1982. It involves covering the tank in explosive boxes called *kostek* (dice) that blow a steel plate into the path of an incoming shaped-charge warhead. This dissipates its penetrating power.

T-55AM-1 (Model 1983/1988)

This was a T-55A upgrade with Bastion, additional passive armour protection and the V-46-5M engine. Those tanks with the reactive armour and V-46 engine upgrade were designated T-55MV-1 and T-55AMV-1. During 1984–9 Czechoslovakia, East Germany and Poland conducted upgrade programmes in parallel with the Soviet T-55M/T-55AM upgrades. These were designated the T-55AM2 without Bastion and the T-55AM2B with Bastion.

T-55AD (Model 1983/1988)

T-55M upgrade with the then top secret *Drozd* anti-missile system. Incoming threats are detected by a motion sensor that triggers one of eight launch tubes, four either side of the turret, which fires a shotgun blast to take out incoming missiles. Because it was so expensive only 250 were produced for the Soviet Naval Infantry. A few were exported.

T-55AD-1 (Model 1983/1989)

T-55M upgrade with the *Drozd* system and the V-46-5M engine.

Colour Schemes and Camouflage

In common with other Soviet tanks of the Cold War period, T-54/55s were painted dark olive green, with white three-digit tactical numbers and unit symbols on their turrets. This was a hangover from the Second World War when the Red Army dispensed with early efforts at camouflaging their armour.

During the Soviet invasion of Czechoslovakia in 1968, Soviet T-54s featured a distinctive white cross painted over the upper surface including the turret, glacis and engine deck. This was to avoid confusion with Czechoslovakian T-54/55s. The turret call sign number was white, while a white box left of this contained the vehicle number, just below which were the battalion and company numbers.

Those operated by other Warsaw Pact countries were in a similar colour but marked with national identification emblems. The East Germans and the Romanians used distinctive camouflage patterns. East German T-55s employed a three-tone scheme of olive green, medium grey and dark grey, while Romanian TR-85s sported green, brown and black.

Those supplied to the Arab armies tended to painted varying shades of desert sand, though Syrian tanks deployed to the Beka'a Valley in Lebanon and on the Golan Heights were camouflaged with blotches of sand and grey over olive green. Iraqi T-54/55s were often plain sand though during the Iran-Iraq War and the Gulf War some sported a two-tone camouflage of dark green and sand.

During the various wars in Yugoslavia in the 1990s captured pale green T-55s of the Yugoslav National Army were rebadged and repainted by their new owners. The Slovenes' territorial forces hand-painted TO (*Teritorialna Obramba*) in white onto their tanks. The Croats camouflaged some of theirs with reddish brown and black and painted the Croat red-and-white chequerboard shield on the glacis and turret sides. T-55s serving with the elite Croatian Tiger Brigade were haphazardly oversprayed with lime green, dark green and black. Their tiger's head emblem was applied to the turret either side of the main armament. Similarly, tanks of the Bosnian Croat's Army's 1st Guards Brigade had a blotchy four-colour camouflage scheme, with white tactical numbers on the turret and glacis. A gold-on-black insignia was painted on the turret either side of the main gun.

Pakistan's Chinese-supplied Type 59s were photographed in a very dark green with patches of pale grey or sand camouflage. In Uganda two Polish-built T-55s, photographed in Kampala in 1976 during a military parade to mark Idi Amin's fifth anniversary in power, had an unusual stippling affect and very short stripes painted over the green, with the turret numbers '739' and '755'.

Opposite above: Soviet T-55s, clearly lacking the turret ventilator dome and the loader's cupola. These are probably Model 1961 versions and have the Luna infra-red searchlight. This shows how exposed the commander and driver are with their hatches open.

Opposite below: Bosnian inspectors examining a Polish-built T-55 belonging to the Serbian 125th Motorized Brigade at Kruševac in 2006.

T-55s on exercise with supporting infantry. The T-55A Model 1961 was fitted with an NBC protection system.

Polish-built T-55 belonging to the Iraqi Army lost on the Kuwait-Basra Highway in 1991. The loader's hatch is fitted with the anti-aircraft MG mounting. Its captors have daubed the whole tank in graffiti.

This training cutaway of a T-55 turret shows just how cramped the fighting compartment is. The commander, gunner, and loader all have to operate in this confined space.

One of the main armament ammunition racks is located just to the right of the driver and the bow machine gun.

Close-up of one of the ammunition racks – the T-54 can carry a total of thirty-four 100mm rounds and the T-55 some forty-three rounds.

Two types of 109cm long 100-44 D-10 tank gun drill rounds. The first has a brass outer casing with solid steel warhead, the other steel with wood.

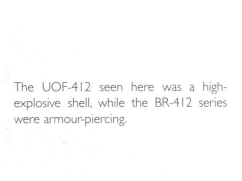

The UOF-412 seen here was a high-explosive shell, while the BR-412 series were armour-piercing.

A T-55AD with the *Drozd* anti-missile system. This was the very first active protection system for a tank. The launcher fires a fragmentation warhead to destroy any incoming threat.

Afghan T-55 Model 1970 or T-55A (1970) laid up for the winter. The T-54/55 saw extensive action in Afghanistan during the Soviet-Afghan War.

Hull-down Iraqi T-55 destroyed during Operation Desert Storm in 1991. Interestingly the loader's hatch is mounted on a cupola.

Mujahedeen with a captured Afghan T-55 photographed in the 1980s.

Northern Alliance troops with a T-55 during Operation Enduring Freedom launched in 2001 to topple the Taliban.

Another Iraqi T-55 lost during the 1991 Gulf War.

The T-55 was essentially the same as the T-54 with internal changes that included a more powerful engine and larger ammunition stowage.

T-55s serving with the Croatian armed forces that once belonged to the Yugoslav National Army. The nearest has a three-tone camouflage scheme and both have the Croat red-and-white chequerboard badge.

Chapter Four

T-54/55
Specialized Variants

The T-54/55 was utilized in a wide variety of specialized variants by the Soviet and the Warsaw Pact armies, including armoured recovery, bridgelaying, command, flamethrower, mineclearer and self-propelled anti-aircraft guns. The following lists some of the more common Soviet types; foreign-built gun tanks and their variants are covered in the following chapter.

T-54 Specialized Variants

T-54-T Armoured Recovery Vehicle

This was the initial designation for the turretless T-54 armoured recovery vehicle (ARV), which was fitted with a very wide snorkel tube to ford deep rivers and appeared in the 1950s. Subsequently at least half-a-dozen types of T-54/55 ARVs were developed. Most had limited capabilities compared to their Western counterparts and were mainly intended to tow damaged vehicles off the battlefield. These were known as *Bronetankoviy Tyagach Srdniy* (BTS – medium armoured tractors).

The T-54-T/T-55-T was the first model to enter service and performed a similar role to the T-34-T (B) ARV, though it was based on a more powerful chassis. This had a loading platform in the centre of the vehicle, with sides that could be folded down to permit unloading or loading of replacement engines or transmissions. A jib crane was also provided along with a large spade mounted at the rear of the hull.

BTS Armoured Recovery Vehicle

The BTS-1 was the first version of the T-55 to be used as an ARV consisting of the T-54A with the turret removed. There were at least four variants with different weight-lifting equipment. The BTS-2 was fitted with a winch and large anchoring spade at the rear to assist with tank recovery. It was also equipped with a small tripod jib crane. This ARV was produced in Czechoslovakia as the WZT-1.

Appearing in the 1960s, the BTS-3 (also designated the SPK-12G) featured a hydraulic crane fitted to the front left of the hull, with a telescopic jib enabling the vehicle to lift tank engines and turrets. The vehicle was additionally equipped with a front-mounted BTU-55 dozer blade, rear-mounted spade and a winch. The BTS-4 was similar to the BTS-2 but with the crane pivoted on the left side of the hull with a telescopic jib.

On all the variants the vehicle commander was normally seated to the right at the front of the hull, served by a single-piece hatch that opened to the right. To his left was seated the driver who was provided with two periscopes for observation and a single-piece hatch cover. The mechanics normally rode in the cargo hold, though this was uncomfortable as it also contained their tools, the snorkel when it was stowed and spare fuel drums.

T-54/MTU-1 Bridgelayer

The *Tankoviy Mostoukladchik* (MTU – bridgelayer tank) comprised a turretless T-54 carrying a 12m-long rigid bridge (capable of spanning 11m) mounted on a launch frame. The MTU-1 entered service with the Soviet Army in the late 1950s. The bridge was constructed from four box truss panels, with inner treadways for small vehicles and outer ones for tracked vehicles. When on the move the inner treadway ramp sections were folded on top of the main treadways.

It took a maximum of five minutes to launch the bridge. When an obstacle that needed crossing was reached the span was winched forward on the launching frame employing a chain drive mechanism, the latter being disengaged once the bridge was firmly lowered into place. The bridge could take up to 50 tonnes and could be recovered after use from either end.

For protection the vehicle was armed with a 12.7mm DShKM machine gun. This was positioned between the two treadways in the centre of the hull. In order to lay the bridge the weapon had to be removed. The MTU-1 bridgelayer only required a two-man crew. Late production models also utilized the T-55 chassis.

T-54K Command Tank

This was the first standard command version of the T-54A (Model 1955) fitted with additional radios sets. To accommodate the extra communications equipment meant a reduction in ammunition carried. Other command models included the T-54AK and the T-54BK. The T54-AK-1, equipped with a second R-113 radio, was designed for company commanders. The AK-2 was for battalion and regimental commanders as well as regimental chiefs-of-staff. On this variant the HTM-10 telescopic antenna mast increased the broadcast range.

T-54/BTU Dozer

The T-54 could be converted into a bulldozer or *Buldozer Tankoviy Universalniy* (BTU

– universal tank dozer) with the installation of a 3.4m-wide dozer blade onto the nose plate. It was intended for emplacing tanks or breaching anti-tank obstacles. Fitting though was time-consuming and could take up to 90 minutes to attach and up to 60 minutes to remove.

OT-54 Flamethrower

The 7.62mm coaxial machine gun was replaced by the ATO-1 automatic flamethrower (derived from the Second World War ATO-41/42 which was hull-mounted in the T-34). Ammunition storage in the bow was altered to permit the tank to carry 460 litres of flammable liquid. This was fired using compressed air, providing up to twenty bursts out to a range of 160m. Accepted into service in 1954, it was only built in very limited quantities. The T-54B was also used as the basis for a flamethrower tank in 1959 but on this variant the flame gun replaced the main armament.

T-54 Mineclearer

This variant consisted of a T-54 fitted with the PT-54 mine roller system, which was very similar in design to the earlier P-34 used on the T-34/76 and T-34/85 tanks in the Second World War. A framework holding two sets of six serrated rollers was fixed to the front of the hull. These wheels are aligned with the tank's tracks so the area between the tracks remained uncleared. The modified PT-54M featured sets of five rollers rather than six. Another version used two serrated ploughs which were lighter and did not impede the tank's cross-country mobility.

SU-122 Tank Destroyer

In 1949, following on from their experiences with tank destroyers during the Second World War, the Soviets produced the SU-122 (also known as the IT-122). This comprised a T-54 chassis with a superstructure very similar to the T-34-derived SU-100 tank destroyer. Mounted in the front of the hull was a 122mm gun with very limited traverse and elevation. The SU-122s were withdrawn from service in the late 1950s and reconfigured as armoured recovery vehicles which NATO designated the M1977. This was achieved by simply removing the gun and covering the mantlet aperture in the glacis plate.

ZSU-57-2 self-propelled anti-aircraft gun

The *Zenitnaya Samokhodnaya Ustanovka* (ZSU – anti-aircraft self-propelled mount) consisted of a shortened T-54 chassis with only four road wheels, fitted with an open-topped turret containing twin 57mm anti-aircraft guns. This had a full 360-degree traverse and carried 316 rounds of ready-use ammunition in clips of four rounds. This was a clear-weather, line-of-sight weapons system that was soon replaced by the vastly more versatile radar-directed ZSU-23-4 based on the PT-76 amphibious light tank.

T-55 Specialized Variants
T-55 MTU-20 Bridgelayer
The MTU-20 was based on the T-55 chassis rather than the T-54. This entered service in the late 1960s as a replacement for the MTU-1. It had a 20m bridge (capable of spanning 18m), the ends of which folded back to lie on top of the bridge to reduce the overall length when in transit. Like its predecessor it took just five minutes to deploy or recover and only required two crew to operate.

T-55 Combat Engineer Vehicle
The *Inzhenernaia Maschina Razgrazheniia* (IMR – combat engineer vehicle) comprised a turretless T-55 with a hydraulically-operated crane that could traverse 360 degrees. The crane could take a pair of pincher grabs for lifting or a small bucket for digging. Night operations were facilitated by the provision of a searchlight mounted on the crane. An armoured cupola with observation windows provided protection for the crane operator. At the front was a dozer blade that could be used in either a straight or V configuration. The IMR first appeared in the early 1970s.

T-55K Command Vehicle
The T-55K carried less ammunition than a regular gun tank in order to accommodate additional communications equipment and a generator. This enabled it to act as a command tank, of which there were at least three versions that featured different radios. The K1 and K2 carried two R-132 or R-123M and one R-124 radios. The T-55K3 was equipped with one R-123M, R-124 and R-130M plus a 10m antenna. Subsequent variants were dubbed the T-55AK and T-55MK.

T-55/BTU Dozer
The BTU-55 had a redesigned and lighter type of dozer blade, and at 1.4 tonnes compared to the BTU's 2.3 tonnes it was the more commonplace of the two. It was also slightly quicker to fit and remove than the earlier design. Notably there was not a bulldozer for the T-62, though the T-64 and T-72 could incorporate a dozer blade for self-emplacement.

TO-55 Flamethrower
The AT-200 flame-gun was used to arm the T-55 flamethrower. The flame gun was again installed in place of the coaxial machine gun and was fired by one of twelve pyrotechnic cartridges carried by the tank. While fuelled by the same quantity of flammable liquid as the earlier OT-54, the subsequent OT-55 had a longer range of

200m. This was the most common Soviet flamethrower tank and was used by the Soviet Army and Naval Infantry.

T-55 Mineclearer

The T-55 was modified to take the PT-55 mine roller system in 1959. Attachment fittings were welded to the hull front to take the 6-ton PT-55. This only had four rollers in each section so cleared a narrower path. Its weight was such that the roller was only installed when the tank was specifically on mineclearing operations. The PT-54/55 took about five minutes to detach and could survive the blast of ten swept anti-tank mines.

The KMT-4 tank-mounted mineclearing plough was introduced in the 1960s, comprising a 600mm wide cutting device with five cutting tines mounted at an angle in front of each track. These were lowered by hydraulic ram and simply ploughed up mines for removal rather than detonating them. This was followed by the KMT-5 that combined the plough and rollers. The latter were a new design and only had three rollers per section. Both had a quick release mechanism which allowed the driver to drop them rapidly. However, the plough and rollers could not be used simultaneously unless the ground was very flat, so were deployed depending what type of ground or minefield they were required to clear. The KMT-4/5 were compatible with the T-55 and T-62.

T-55 BMR Mineclearer

In the 1980s the Soviet Army deployed a turretless T-55 mineclearing vehicle to Afghanistan. This was believed to be a variant of the M1977 Armoured Recovery Vehicle (see below) converted to take a mineclearing plough with the KMT-5 or KMT-7 roller system. The driver was seated on the left with the commander to his right. The latter was served by a cupola mounting a 12.7mm machine gun while on the right side of the hull was a bank of smoke grenade dischargers firing forward. While in Afghanistan the BMR mainly deployed the mineclearing rollers to avoid the ploughs tearing up the country's rudimentary roads to the extent that wheeled vehicles could not use the cleared path.

SU-130 Tank Destroyer

In the 1950s T-55 chassis were used to create the IT-130 tank destroyer armed with a modified 130mm M-46 field gun. Similar in appearance to the SU-100, only a small number were produced. This conversion did not prove very successful and like the IT-122 was converted into an armoured recovery vehicle in the late 1950s known as the M1977 ARV. These were not equipped with winches or any other recovery equipment so were restricted to a towing role, thereby limiting their utility. During the 1980s some of these were used as ad hoc armoured mineclearing vehicles.

The Soviet-built T-54 MTU-1 bridgelayer was introduced in 1958 to replace an older one based on the T-34. Later versions used the T-55 chassis as well. It took just five minutes to position the bridge.

The Soviet IMR was first seen in 1973 and was based on a T-55 chassis. It is equipped with a hydraulic crane with pincher grabs and a dozer blade. Note the large armoured cupola for the crane operator that enabled the vehicle to deploy whilst under fire.

Czechoslovak VT-55A ARV – this example is missing its dozer blade. It is based on the T-55A MBT chassis while an earlier Czech version, the MT-55, drew on the T-55-T ARV.

Polish T-55 supported by the IWT, the Polish version of the IMR.

Iraqi T-54/55s or Type 59/69s lost in 2003. Two types of armoured recovery vehicle can be seen either side of the road. The furthest-away appears to be a Chinese Type 653.

Czech-built MT-55A armoured bridgelayer in travelling configuration – this utilizes a turretless T-55A MBT chassis carrying a scissor bridge. This was exported to at least half a dozen countries including Iraq.

Column of Warsaw Pact T-55s on exercise supported by MT-55As.

Front view of the MT-55 showing the electro-hydraulic system used for launching the bridge into position.

BLG-60 armoured bridgelayer on a Soviet *Gusenichniy Samokhodniy Parom* (GSP – heavy amphibious ferry). This was a version of the MT-55 built in East Germany for the East German and Polish Armies.

Serbian ZSU-57-2 photographed in 1996. During the Balkan Wars these guns were also used in a ground support role against enemy positions.

The ZSU-57-2 self-propelled anti-aircraft gun utilized a shorted T-54 chassis armed with twin 57mm guns. This only had four road wheels rather than the standard five.

Remains of a North Vietnamese ZSU-57-2 lost during the Vietnam War. The turret is in the reverse position.

All the various turretless armoured recovery variants built by the Soviet Union and other Warsaw Pact countries were essentially the same as the VT-55A. However, they had varying levels of equipment fitted depending on what tasks they were required to fulfil.

Chapter Five

Warsaw Pact Copies

While the Soviet Union built around 50,000 T-54/55s, the Non-Soviet Warsaw Pact (NSWP) states produced another 17,000, many of which were exported. After 1945 the Soviet Union was keen to rearm its new-found allies in Eastern Europe as well as emerging communist governments around the world. By the time of the collapse of the Soviet Union in 1991 there were still thousands of foreign-built T-54/55s in service in Europe.

Czechoslovakia

After the war Czechoslovakia was soon put to work producing the tried and tested T-34/85 medium tank and the SU-100 tank destroyer. Most of these were sent to the Middle East to equip the Arab armies in their wars against Israel. Then the Czechoslovaks began to build the T-54/55 for both domestic use and the export markets, totalling at least 8,500 tanks. This was followed by the T-72.

Between 1958 and 1966 Czechoslovakia produced 2,855 T-54As and 120 T-54AK command variants at the ZTS Martin tank plant. Also from 1958 to 1982 the plant built 3,820 T-55As, 3,377 T-55s and 1,280 T-55AK1 command tanks. Many of these were sent overseas. By the early 1990s Czechoslovakia still had 1,547 T-54s and 1,543 T-55s in its tank fleet. While the Czech T-54s were viewed as superior to those built by the Soviets, Moscow appears to have had a hand in their production. Notably, some surviving Czech T-54s are kitted out with Soviet-made electrics, gauges, optics and radios.

The Czechoslovak T-54/55s were modernized to produce the T-55AM2. The modifications included full-length track skirts which covered the upper part of the track. The 100mm gun was fitted with a thermal sleeve, and passive armour was added to the front of the turret (similar to that fitted on Soviet T-62s). Forward-firing smoke grenade dischargers were installed on the rear of the turret to the right-hand side

Poland

Initially the Polish tank plant at Bumar-Labedy went into production in 1951 also building the T-34/85, the production run of which ended three years later. This was followed by 2,855 T-54As from 1956 to 1964 and the T-55 from 1958 until 1979. In total the Poles built 8,570 T-54/55s, many of which were issued to other Warsaw Pact armies and exported to the Developing World. Poland, like Czechoslovakia, then switched to producing the T-72. The Polish equivalent of the T-54B (Model 1957) was the T-54AM, a designation sometimes used for both Polish and Soviet models of this type.

Production of the D-10 tank gun was also undertaken in Czechoslovakia and Poland. It was probably built in former Yugoslavia as well. In Poland the 100mm D-10T2S was produced by Huta Stalowa Wola SA. Czechoslovak and Polish T-55s capable of firing the Bastion anti-tank missiles were known as the T-55AM2B and T-55AM2P respectively. The Czech version used the Kladivo laser rangefinder rather than the standard Soviet KTD-2, mounted over the main armament. The Polish tanks utilized the Merida fire-control system with the laser rangefinder integrated with the gunner's sight.

The Poles also produced a command or *dowodca* version of the T-54A designated the T-54D. To accommodate the extra communications equipment, it had a modified turret with a slight extension at the year. It was issued to regimental commanders and their chiefs of staff. A similar Polish T-55 version was also built.

Polish-built T-54/55 tanks are easily distinguishable from Soviet ones by the large rectangular stowage box on the left side of the turret. In addition, on the Polish and Czech models the cover fitting on the gunner's telescope opening to the left of the main armament is more oval than on its Soviet counterparts. Many NSWP tanks were subsequently upgraded by their various operators with additional armour and computerized fire-control systems. Poland still had 1,758 T-55s in the early 1990s, Hungary over 1,100, Romania around 760 and Bulgaria 1,280

Romania

While the Romanians, like the Czechs and Poles, built a copy of the T-55 they also went one step further and redesigned it producing a somewhat modified version. While Czechoslovakia and Poland both had a history of producing tanks that dated from before the Second World War, Romania did not and the sharp learning curve was to cause it problems.

Locally-built Romanian T-55s were first seen in 1977 and were designated the TR-77 (or M1977 by the West). However, these may have been manufactured earlier. In light of Romania having no experience in tank manufacturing these T-55s may have been supplied by Moscow as knock-down kits which the Romanians assembled. Subsequent Romanian modified versions of the TR-77 included the TR-580, TR-85 and the TM-800 though it is unclear if the latter went into series production.

The TR-580 was powered by a 432.5kW/580hp engine, hence its designation, and entered service in 1982.

It was armed with the standard 100mm gun with fume extractor, though it lacked a laser rangefinder. The hull and chassis was similar to the T-55 but it was lengthened to allow for six unique spoked road wheels, with a gap between the first and second ones, either side, whereas the T-55 had five. To allow for this modification a single return roller was also installed. The T-54/55 type exhaust outlet was kept above the last two road-wheel stations on the left-hand side and the rear engine decking remained similar to the standard T-55. The upper part of the front idler, road wheels and rear drive sprocket were covered by steel skirts which angled up at either end.

Romania then produced the TR-85, which entered service in 1987. This also had six road wheels – with a distinct gap between the first/second, second/third and fifth/sixth wheels, again with the drive sprocket at the rear and idler at the front. It did not have the exhaust outlet on the left-hand side that is a standard feature of the T-54/T-55. This tank had a new German-built 641.3kW/860hp diesel engine that required modification of the rear hull compartment and decking. As a result the engine compartment top differed from that of the T-54/55 series. This new engine gave it a top speed of 60km/hr and a 310km range.

Like its predecessors the TR-85 was armed with a 100mm gun, with a fume extractor near the muzzle and a thermal sleeve. A rangefinder like that fitted to the Chinese Type 69 was mounted above the mantlet. Installed on the forward left-hand side of the turret was a rectangular stowage box very similar to that on the Polish-built T-55. The commander, gunner and driver were provided with a full range of infra-red night vision equipment. The TR-85, however, had a troubled production and proved to be mechanically unreliable, in part because it weighed almost 50 tons, over 11 tons heavier than the TR-580. The Romanian leader Nicolae Ceauşescu was so alarmed at the quality that he almost cancelled the TR-85 programme.

Some of these Romanian-built tanks were involved in the attempt to stop the uprising that toppled Ceauşescu in 1989. The prototype TM-800 appeared in 1994 and was thought to be an export version of the TR-580. This featured a computerized fire-control system and laser rangefinder. The prototype had new laminate armour which came at a cost as it pushed the tank's weight to over 44 tons making it almost as heavy as the TR-85. In the early 1990s Romania still had over 600 TR-85s and over 400 TR-580s. A number of improved versions were developed including the TR-85M1 and the TR-85N which were uparmoured. A distinguishing feature of the M1 is that it has two return rollers.

NSWP Specialized Variants
Czechoslovakia, East Germany, Finland and Poland all produced specialized versions

of the T-55. The VT-55A ARV was Czech-built with a pivoted crane on the right-hand side of the hull rear and a forward mounted dozer blade. The latter was hydraulically operated. Forward of the cargo carrying area was a distinctive cupola on the forward right side. The VT-55 has two winches, one run off the main engine and the other hydraulic. An earlier version known as the MT-55 lacked the dozer blade. The Poles produced their own variant of the T-55 combat engineer vehicle known as the *inzynieryjiny woz torujacy* (IWT). The IWT, while similar to the Czech version, also carried a mineclearing rocket system that was fitted on the Polish Army's T-55s.

The East Germans developed at least three types of T-54/55 ARV. These comprised the T-54 (A), (B) and (C). The first was equipped with a push/pull bar, a dismountable crane with a weightlifting capacity of 1 tonne and a fording snorkel. It did not have a winch or rear spade. It was also designed to take the PT-54/55 mine roller. The only difference with the second vehicle was that it had towing brackets fitted at the rear. The T-54 (C) was re-designated the T-55-TK and was equipped with a dozer blade, rear spade, heavy duty crane, stowage platform and snorkel. The crane had a telescopic jib and could lift 20 tonnes.

Also known as the MT-55 was the Czech-designed bridgelayer. This was developed to replace the earlier MT-34 which was based on the T-34 tank chassis. The MT-55 carried a scissor bridge that was launched hydraulically over the front of the hull. Once extended this was 18m and could span a 16m gap. Poland produced as least two bridgelayers based on the T-54/55 chassis, known as the WZT-1 and WZT-2. These were equivalent to the Soviet BTS-2 and BTS-3 respectively. East Germany and Poland developed the BLG-60 bridgelayer as a replacement for the MT-55.

Opposite: A heavily-camouflaged Polish-built T-55 that has just driven off a GSP heavy amphibious ferry. The national recognition symbol is visible on the front of the turret.

Czechoslovak-built T-54. The Czechs, Poles and Romanians all produced their own versions of the T-54/55 during the Cold War with slight variations.

Polish T-54As on manoeuvres. The Poles built 2,855 T-54As from 1956 to 1964.

Polish T-55s. Note the very large storage box on the left side of the turret, this was a particular Polish feature. Another distinctive feature on the Polish T-55 is the prominent combing around the turret hatches which housed anti-radiation lining.

The gunner's sight opening on the turret of Polish and Czech-built tanks is much more oval than on its Soviet counterparts, as can be seen on this Polish T-55.

The turret on this Czech-built T-54 also has the distinctive cast oval cover fitting round the gunner's sight aperture plus a lower bracket.

The oval cover fitting and lower bracket are welded to the turret. The latter does not appear on Polish-built T-54/55s.

East German T-55 using its wading snorkel. East Germany declined to convert to the T-62 and relied on the T-54/55 until the late 1980s when it introduced the T-72.

Polish T-55s. The loader is manning the 12.7mm DShKM anti-aircraft machine gun. Note the tank fitted with the mine plough just to the right.

This Czech-built T-54 has its full complement of spare fuel tanks and smoke canisters. Limited internal space meant that when in the field equipment had to be stored on the outside of the tank as well. The narrow black oblong shape on the track guard just behind the long stowage bin is the exhaust outlet.

Polish-built East German T-55AM2B with reinforced glacis armour, turret brow armour and laser rangefinder over main gun, plus rubber side skirts.

Warsaw Pact T-55s on exercise – the badge on these tanks is white, green and red indicating they may belong to the Bulgarian Army.

Romanian TR-85 showing the six-wheel configuration and single return roller. It has the Chinese-style laser rangefinder and Polish turret stowage box.

The modernized version of the TR-85, known as the M1, with redesigned turret and twin return rollers. It retained the 100mm gun. Very few of these upgrades were carried out.

Chapter Six

Chinese Cousins

After Mao Zedong and the communists took power in China in 1949 they obtained several hundred Soviet T-34/85s. These were used to equip a single mechanized division. After some delay the Chinese began to produce a copy designated the Type 58, but this was swiftly redundant with the appearance of the T-54. It is not clear if the Chinese ever had a full manufacturing capability for the T-34/85 like the Czechs and Poles, or simply conducted sub-assembly and refurbishments.

Initial Chinese perceptions of the utility of the tank were greatly influenced by their experiences in Korea and Indochina. In Korea the terrain had confined the North Korean tanks to the roads and they had proved vulnerable to enemy air attack. General Wei Guoqing, the chief Chinese advisor to the Viet Minh in Indochina, had witnessed how they had defeated the French without recourse to tanks. China's most significant contribution to the Viet Minh's war effort had been artillery and anti-aircraft guns, not tanks. The French had employed the M24 Chaffee light tank and the M4 Sherman medium tank which had given then little discernible strategic advantage.

Many senior Chinese generals saw little scope for the tank in the 'people's war' again the capitalists. They were steeped in the tradition of the 'human wave' attack, as used during the Chinese Civil War and the Korean War. Besides, the neighbouring Soviet Union was a fellow communist state so there was no threat from that quarter – or so the Chinese thought.

In the 1950s Moscow supplied the People's Republic of China with a number of T-54As. The Chinese subsequently built their own version, the 36-ton Type 59 MBT that appeared in late 1957. These were constructed by Factory N.617 in Baotou in Chinese Inner Mongolia. The Chinese selected the location because it was a city built up around heavy industry, in particular steel. In addition being close to Mongolia meant that it was remote. Once Baotou became the site of a plutonium plant the Chinese had to disperse their tank-building facilities for fear of nuclear attack by America or the Soviet Union.

The early-model Type 59 looked almost identical to the T-54 but was not equipped with a main armament stabilizer or infra-red night vision equipment. Later models were fitted with a fume extractor similar to the T-54A, an infra-red searchlight for the commander and gunner plus a larger one above the main gun, with a laser rangefinder just to the right of it. To arm the Type 59 China produced a copy of the D-10T tank gun but the Chinese designation for this weapon is not known.

Type 59 Main Battle Tank

Subsequent upgrades resulted in the Type 59-I and Type 59-II, the latter being armed with a 105mm rifled gun. Outwardly the Type 59-I was the same but featured a simplified fire-control system and laser rangefinder, plus low pressure engine alarm and an automatic fire extinguisher. Also the cupola door cover and safety door cover were fitted with a hydraulic booster to improve opening and closing. On the Type 59-II the barrel was fitted with a distinctive fume extractor and thermal sleeve. The Chinese produced up to 700 Type 59 a year by the 1970s, rising to a rate of about 1,000 a year by the early 1980s.

Type 59 Armoured Recovery Vehicle

This consisted of a Type 59 with its turret removed. As it did not have a winch, it functioned purely as a towing vehicle. Armament was provided by a single 12.7mm machine gun. It is thought this ARV may have been a field modification rather than factory built.

Type 62 Light Tank

A derivative of the Type 59 was the Type 62 light tank, developed to cope with China's harsher environments, especially hilly terrain and soft ground where the former could not operate. This was essentially a scaled-down version with slightly smaller dimensions and from a distance it was hard to tell the two apart. The layout was identical to the Type 59. The designers ensured the tank, armed with a shorter 85mm gun, had lower ground pressure and was 15 tons lighter than the Type 59. About 800 were built for the Chinese People's Liberation Army (PLA) and around 500 for export.

Type 62 Armoured Recovery Vehicle

Some of the light tank variant were converted into armoured recovery vehicles. It is not clear if these were production vehicles or simply field conversions.

Type 63 Light Amphibious Tank

The Chinese Type 63 was based on the Soviet PT-76 light amphibious tank, so the hull and wheels bear no resemblance to the T-54. However, the Chinese version is noteworthy as it featured a turret similar to the Type 62 and was likewise armed with the same 85mm gun. Its roof though was flatter, had smaller commander/loader hatch mountings, no ventilator dome and single handrails either side. About 1,200 were built for the Chinese Army and a number were exported to North Korea and North Vietnam.

Thanks to regular border wars with India and the Soviet Union the Chinese had need of both the Type 62 and Type 63. The frontier with India is dominated by the Himalayas so is not tank country. In contrast the border to the north-east with the Soviet Union along the Ussuri River is very marshy territory.

Type 69 Main Battle Tank

A further development of the Chinese Type 59 was the Type 69 that appeared publicly in 1982, though it may as its designation implies have gone into service some years earlier. The differences in appearance between the two were minimal. It drew on the Soviet T-62, an example of which was captured in 1969, though it did not copy the latter's 115mm gun. The Type 69 had a infra-red/white light headlamp arrangement that differed from that on Soviet tanks.

It also had distinctive cage-like 'boom shields' or 'grid shields' on the turret sides and rear as well as a bank of four smoke grenade dispensers on either side of the turret. The 'boom shields', consisting of metal louvres mounted 450mm from the turret, were designed to detonate HEAT warheads and developed as a result of experience in the 1979 war with Vietnam. Side skirts were also fitted to protect the upper track. Another distinctive feature was a semi-circular protrusion on the bottom of the rear hull plate to allow for a new fan copied from the Soviet T-62.

Although the Type 69 drew on improvements featured on the Soviet T-62, it remained closer to the T-54 in design. The Type 69-I was armed with a smoothbore 100mm gun (this was slightly longer than the 100mm rifled bore on the Type 59 and has a bore evacuator near the end of the muzzle), while the Type 69-II had the rifled 100mm gun and a different fire-control system. The first variant does not seem to have been very successful and was superseded by the second model after just 150 Type 69-Is had been delivered. A Type 69-III or Type 79 was produced for the export market armed with a 105mm gun, but only just over 500 were ever built.

Type 653 Armoured Recovery Vehicle

This vehicle was produced to provide battlefield support for the Type 69 main battle tank. Whereas the Type 59 ARV was only a towing vehicle the Type 653 was much more capable. It could not only recover stranded tanks, but also conduct major repairs such as replacing engines, remove obstacles and digging firing positions for gun tanks and artillery.

It comprised a Type 69 hull and chassis minus the turret. In place of the latter to left a fixed superstructure was installed, while to the right was a hydraulic crane. The latter was mounted on a 360-degree turntable situated in line with the driver's position. A hydraulic dozer blade could be fitted to the front. The main winch enabled it to haul up to 70 tonnes. The Type 653 required a five-man crew.

Type 84 Bridgelayer

This likewise consisted of a Type 69 with its turret removed and replaced with bridge launching system. The bridge of light steel folded in half with one on top of the other when in transit. This extended to 18m and could bridge a 16-metre gap. It could take wheeled and tracked vehicles weighing up to 40 tonnes. A hydraulically-operated stabilizer blade was mounted under the front of the hull and this was employed during the last phase of bridgelaying; it could also be used as a dozer blade. The Type 84 required three crew including the driver.

Type 80 Self-Propelled Anti-Aircraft Gun

This was the Chinese version of the Soviet ZSU-57-2. It utilized a modified Type 69-II equipped with an open-topped turret armed with twin 57mm cannon. This had a vertical range of 8,000m, though it was only effective to 5,000m, and a horizontal range of 12,000m. The Type 80 had a six-man crew. During the 1980s the Chinese also built several prototypes armed with twin 37mm guns but these did not go into production.

Considerable quantities of Type 59/69s were cynically exported to both Tehran and Baghdad during the Iran-Iraq War. Pakistan also proved to be a major customer for both models – these though proved unreliable – as well as Thailand and Zimbabwe. Small numbers of the Type 653 ARV were also supplied to Bangladesh, Iraq, Pakistan and Thailand. Drawing on these tank designs the Chinese went on to produce the Type 79, 80, 85 and 90 tanks. The Type 85-II was also built for the Pakistani Army. China produced somewhere in the region of 10,000 Type 59/69s.

Opposite above: Soviet-supplied T-34/85s on parade in Beijing with the Chinese People's Liberation Army in 1950. China attempted to produce its own version known as the Type 58.

Opposite below: The Chinese subsequently copied the T-54, producing their Type 59/69 MBTs. The initial Type 59, seen here, was essentially the same as the T-54A, while the Type 59-1 featured some internal changes and was fitted with a laser rangefinder.

The Chinese-built Type 59 retained the T-54's characteristic mushroom ventilator dome as well as the commander and loader's cupolas.

Type 59-IIs armed with 105mm guns. Although the mid-barrel fume extractor is clearly visible these examples do not have thermal sleeves. In 1991 Saddam Hussein ordered up to 600 Type 59s for the Iraqi Army.

The Type 62 light tank was a scaled-down, lighter version of the Type 59 armed with an 85mm gun, which had a much shorter barrel.

Like the Type 59, the Type 62 retained the T-54's turret ventilator dome and general layout.

The Chinese Type 63 light amphibious tank used a turret similar to the Type 62, but with a flatter roof, no ventilator dome and single handrails either side.

The Type 63 hull and chassis was based on the Soviet PT-76. Note the smaller turret hatch mountings compared to the Type 62 to the right.

Chinese Type 69-II supplied to the Iraqi Army. Note the laser rangefinder on the top edge of the 100mm gun's mantlet. This was vulnerable to shell splinters and small-arms fire.

The Type 69 has a different headlamp configuration compared to the T-54 and Type 59. On the latter they are mounted on the glacis plate to the right (facing forward), while the Type 69 has them over the track guards on either side.

Coalition forces examine a Type 69 knocked out by French armour in 1991.

The rear of the same Iraqi Type 69-II. It has the distinctive semicircular edge on the bottom of the rear hull plate. This allowed for the new fan which was copied from the Soviet T-62. The basket frame around the turret was designed to thwart hollow charge weapons.

Remains of an abandoned Iraqi Type 69-II. It retains its turret 'boom shields' but not the side skirts.

Left above: This Iraqi Type 69-II was captured during Desert Storm in 1991 by the US 6th Marines. It lacks its laser rangefinder over the main armament and the side skirts are damaged.

Described as a T-55A outside Kuwait City, this is in fact a Chinese Type 69.

Chapter Seven

Middle-Eastern Upgrades

Inevitably over the years large numbers of T-54/55s were upgraded and retrofitted by their various users. The Israelis captured very considerable quantities during the 1967 and 1973 Arab-Israeli Wars. Initially those still operational were quickly refurbished with Israeli radios, then some had their 100mm gun replaced with a 105mm rifled gun, new ammunition racks and new seats for the commander and gunner. The Soviet-designed machine guns were replaced with American Brownings used by the Israelis.

These Israeli-upgraded tanks were generically dubbed the Ti-67 after the 1967 Six Day War, although the T-54A derivatives are also known as the Tiran 4 and the T-55 as the Tiran 5. Although a welcome stop-gap, understandably these tanks were not popular. The crews disliked them because of the danger of drawing friendly fire and because of the cramped interior. As a result they were mainly employed as a war reserve and did not see much combat.

In the mid-1980s the Israelis announced the T-54/55 Model S upgrade which included their proven Blazer ERA being added to the turret and hull. This in part made the Tiran look more like the Israelis' M60s which were also fitted with Blazer. In addition a number of T-54/55 chassis were converted into armoured personnel carriers known as the Achzarit.

During the 1980s the Iraqis carried out a series of largely experimental enhancements. While the Iraqi Army generally referred to its fleet as T-54/55s, many were in fact Chinese Type 59/69s and Polish-built T-55s. During the Baghdad International Defence Exhibition in 1989 the Iraqis displayed a upgunned Type 69 which was armed with the 125mm smoothbore gun used on the T-72 tank. This had an auto loader that would enable the crew to be reduced to three (commander, gunner and driver). This rearming required raising the roof of the turret as well as the cupolas. The vehicle was also fitted with new side skirts, forward-firing electrically-operated smoke grenade dischargers and passive night vision equipment. It is believed that this conversion was a one-off.

Another Iraqi T-54 was used to create a self-propelled 160mm mortar. This they achieved by removing the turret and creating a superstructure housing for a Soviet

M-160 mortar. This had access doors in the sides and rear, but it is unclear if there was a roof to protect the crew. The mortar was locked in a horizontal position when the vehicle was on the move. Again only a single prototype is thought to have been produced. Another turretless variant had a hydraulically-operated mast on top of which there was an armoured observation cabin. This could be elevated up to 25m.

The Iraqis also experimented with uparmouring their T-55s and Type 69s with appliqué multilayer passive armour fitted to the glacis plates, hull sides and the turret. This was in an attempt to emulate the brow laminate armour of the Soviet T-55M. The only Iraqi Army upgrades encountered during Operation Desert Storm were a few Polish T-55s and Chinese Type 69s with this additional frontal armour. Some of these served with the headquarters units of the 5th Mechanized Division and the 15th Mechanized Brigade that fought at al-Khafji in January 1991. After the 2003 Iraq War a number of Iraqi T-54/55s were refurbished and returned to service. Some of which had passive armour on the turret.

Jumping on the Bandwagon

In response to the vast numbers of T-54/55s shipped into the Middle East, it was not long before countries outside the region began jumping on the bandwagon and offering comprehensive upgrade packages. Several hundred Egyptian T-54/55s and T-62s were upgraded by Germany in the 1970s with the installation of AEG/Telefunken white/infra-red searchlights to the right of the main gun. Some were also equipped with the Iskra laser rangefinder. These were designated the T-55E (Egyptian) Mark 0 that were followed by a number of other versions.

Egypt sought to enhance its tank fleet further and with the assistance of the UK's Royal Ordnance looked at installing the 105mm L7A3 rifled tank gun in the T-54/55. Whereas in Western tanks the gun is loaded from the left, in the T-55 the D-10TS gun is loaded from the right. Therefore the L7 had to be rotated through 180 degrees. This rearming greatly assisted first-round hit probability and enabled the tank to fire the latest high-performance kinetic ammunition.

The Egyptians ordered this upgrade in June 1985 but it is unclear how many, if any, were ever actually carried out. America and Germany also sought upgrade contracts with Egypt but many of their projects fell by the wayside. It has been alleged that the entire programme was simply a ruse by senior Egyptians to be wined and dined by Western defence companies even though the money for the upgrades was never available in the first place. The Ramses II upgrade was delayed for years.

The Indian Army likewise sought to develop an upgrade for its T-54/55 using the 105mm L7. The gun was built in India for the locally-produced Vijayanta tank based on the British Vickers Mk I which appeared in the 1960s, so was readily available.

Most of India's T-54/55s were upgraded and the package was offered for export but no sales were secured. Royal Ordnance offered the L7 to Pakistan for its Type 59 but this proceed no further than a single tank for firing trials. In Pakistani eyes Royal Ordnance was showing a clear conflict of interest by dealing with its military rival India.

In the early 1980s the Soviet Union began to fit its T-62 MBTs with additional passive armour protection. This modification was then applied to the T-55s of the Warsaw Pact armies and designated the T-55AM2. There appear to have been few export customers for this upgrade though the Czech Republic continued offering it into the 1990s in the forlorn hope of making money out of T-54/55 operators.

China decided to upgrade its Type 59 with a retrofit package that replaced the 520hp diesel engine with a 730hp diesel offering greater acceleration in combat. Other improvements included gun stabilization in both elevation and traverse, a new fire-control system and NBC protection. To upgun the Type 59, a 120mm smoothbore gun rearming package was developed. The Chinese also increased the firepower of the Type 59/69 by developing the Type 79 and Type 80 that were essentially the Type 69-III. Both tanks were armed with a 105mm rifled gun and were followed by the Type 85 armed with a 105mm gun and then a 125mm gun, but Middle Eastern customers were not forthcoming.

Arab T-54s captured by the Israeli Defence Forces (IDF) and pressed back into service as the Ti-67 or Tiran 4. Some of these served with the 11th (Reserve) Armoured Brigade in Sinai in 1973.

More Arab tanks captured by the Israelis. These T-55s also served with the IDF as the Tiran 5. Some were later upgunned with a 105mm gun. However, the Tiran was unpopular with its Israeli crews for fear of friendly fire and was kept mainly as an emergency war reserve.

The Israeli Achzarit armoured personnel carrier uses a heavily-converted turretless T-54/55 chassis and entered service in the late 1980s. It can carry a total of ten men including the commander and driver.

Polish-built T-55 upgraded by the Iraqis with additional frontal passive armour designed to protect it from HEAT rounds.

Modified Polish-supplied Egyptian T-55 during Operation Bright Star, the annual joint US/Egyptian military exercise, in 1985. This is believed to be a T-55E Mark 0 fitted with the German AEG/Telefunken white/infra-red searchlights and the Iskra laser rangefinder to the right of the main armament. The T-55 behind it does not have the modification.

The same Egyptian T-55E Mark 0 on the beach. It has a base sand colour with dark green camouflage. This upgrade started in the late 1970s and involved several hundred tanks.

The 100mm DT-10TS gun is loaded from the right, whereas the British 105mm L7 gun is loaded from the left. This meant in order to upgrade the T-54/55 the L7 had to be rotated 180 degrees.

Refurbished Iraqi Army T-55 (it clearly lacks the loader's cupola and ventilator dome), following Operation Iraqi Freedom. The back of the turret has been uparmoured and it retains its infra-red lamps, but the laser rangefinder is missing. The smoke is from the exhaust cowl just to the rear of the long stowage bin.

The turret of this refurbished Iraqi T-55 has been fitted with some sort of passive armour system, that looks similar in size and shape to the shields fitted to the Type 69.

Chapter Eight

Darling of the Left

In Europe the T-54/55 became part of the Soviet Union's repressive armoury that quelled any dissent amongst its communist Warsaw Pact allies. Both the T-34 and T-54 were employed in supressing the 1956 Hungarian uprising in Budapest. The Soviets initially committed the T-34 which proved vulnerable to the Hungarians' Molotov cocktails thrown against the fuel tanks and the engine compartment. The second wave included the brand new T-54, which was not so easy to disable. Nonetheless, a number were lost to Hungarian Molotovs and anti-tank guns.

Embarrassingly for Moscow the Hungarians captured a T-54A which they drove into the grounds of the British embassy. It was found to be a lethal combination of armour and firepower. In addition, it was lighter than the British Centurion and the American M48 Patton. The T-54 was then involved in the East-West confrontation in Berlin in the autumn of 1961 when there was a tense stand-off with American M48 tanks at Checkpoint Charlie. Seven years later the T-54/55 took part in the invasion and occupation of Czechoslovakia. During the 1980s it was also deployed with the Soviet Army to Afghanistan.

African Wars

Like most Soviet weaponry, the T-54/55's simplicity meant it was very easy for Developing World armies to use. The changing dynamics of the Cold War meant that allegiances soon changed as countries sought willing arms suppliers. The T-54/55 became the most common tank to be found in Africa, where it saw widespread combat. It was employed widely in the wars fought in Angola, Ethiopia, Mozambique, Somalia and Sudan from the 1960s to the 1980s.

T-55 tanks from the Soviet Union were first supplied to Sudan in the late 1960s by which time the country was blighted by civil war between the north and south. By the late 1970s the Sudanese Army still had about 130 T-54/55s. When the Portuguese left Angola and Mozambique in 1976 and both countries spiralled into bitter civil war, Moscow supplied their newly-installed Marxist governments with weapons including T-54s to fight the rebels.

In the mid- and late 1980s the Angolan Army deployed some of its 200 T-54/55s against UNITA opposition guerrillas during offensives toward the rebel strongholds at Mavinga and Jamba. Cuban troops, including a Cuban armoured division supporting the Angolan Army also operated the T-54/55 in Angola. The fighting involved the South Africans who supported UNITA as part of its policy to contain the spread of communism in southern Africa. Likewise the Mozambican government had around 100 T-54/55s which it used against the Renamo rebels. Tanzania, Zaire and Zimbabwe obtained limited numbers of Chinese Type 59/69s. The first two countries were also supplied with limited numbers of the Chinese Type 62 light tank.

In North Africa both Algeria and Morocco took delivery of T-54s. About fifty were supplied by the Soviet Union to the Algerians, while the Moroccans got twenty from the Soviet Union and another eighty built in Czechoslovakia during the mid-1960s. The Algerian-backed Polisario guerrillas employed them against the Moroccans during the war for Spanish Morocco in 1976–91. They were also used during the Algerian civil war in the 1990s.

Colonel Gaddafi's Libyan Army deployed the T-55 to Chad during the 1981–7 war but it did not help stave off defeat. Chadian troops overran Gaddafi's oasis base at Ouadi Doum in northern Chad in March 1987, capturing a billion dollars' worth of equipment including some 200 T-55 and T-62 tanks. By 2011 the Libyan Army still had around 500 T-55s in service and over 1,000 T-54/55s in storage. Many of these were used unsuccessfully to try and crush the uprising that toppled Gaddafi from power.

Ethiopia had some 400 such tanks which it deployed during the 1970s in the civil war that saw the Eritreans fighting for independence. By the late 1980s the Ethiopian Army was assessed to have about 600 T-54/55. These did little to counter the Eritreans' growing military confidence, however. They defeated the Ethiopians at Afabet on 19 March 1988, who lost 18,000 men and 50 T-54s. Many of these were then used to help capture the Red Sea port of Massawa in February 1990 which sealed Eritrean independence.

Indo-Pakistan Conflict

In the Indian sub-continent Pakistan's relationship with America and Britain changed when they aided India after the 1962 war with communist China. Three years later the arms embargo against the protagonists after the war between Indian and Pakistan forced the latter into the arms of China and the Soviet Union.

India was supplied with Soviet T-54s in the late 1960s while neighbouring Pakistan obtained both the T-54/55 and the Chinese-built Type 59. These they subsequently used against each other during the 1971 Indo-Pakistan War. In this conflict India was able to muster about 450 T-54/55s while Pakistan had 200 Type 59s and 50 T-55s. These represented a third of the Indian tank force and a quarter of the Pakistanis'.

Inevitably using the same tanks caused unwelcome recognition problems, so the Indians fitted a large dummy fume extractor two-thirds of the way up the gun barrel of their T-54s making it look like an L7 105mm. Also a drum was installed on the rear of the turret to alter the tank's silhouette in the hope of avoiding friendly fire. Examples of this ad hoc conversion were photographed on the outskirts of Dacca and at Chamba.

Pakistani forces operating from West and East Pakistan (Bangladesh) had the problem of fighting a two-front war against their much larger neighbour. Three days after the war broke out India recognized Bangladeshi independence. Western Bangladesh was one of the few places suitable for armoured warfare and it was here that the Indians deployed substantial armour. By 14 December 1971, despite numerous river obstacles, the Indian Army had taken most of East Pakistan and the local Pakistani forces surrendered.

In West Pakistan the Pakistani Army deployed the 1st and 6th Armoured Divisions with the 1st and 2nd Corps to bolster its infantry units. An armoured battle was fought around Zafarwal and Pathankot on 15 and 16 December 1971 south of the Chamba salient involving the 6th Armoured. The Pakistanis lost a considerable number of tanks before the Indian Prime Minister announced a ceasefire. To the south the Pakistani 1st Armoured came to grief at Ramgarh in the soft sands and lost thirty-four tanks. The war was a humiliating defeat for Pakistan which lost control of Bangladesh's resources.

Because India was a much bigger customer and a counterweight to China, the Soviet Union stepped up its arms supplies to Delhi. By the end of the decade the Indian Army could field some 900 T-54/55s. Even by the mid-1990s when it was equipped with the newer T-72 it still had 500 T-55s.

While the Chinese Type 59s delivered to Pakistan reportedly had 'a good degree of finish', their rate of fire was hampered because the main gun lacked a stabilizer and the turret had no power traverse. The armour was also poor, with just 100mm on the turret and 85mm on the hull. The Soviets were perhaps understandably dismissive of the Type 59 with Colonel K. Borisov noting that it did 'not fully meet requirements, since [it] possesses inadequate manoeuvrability . . .'.

Nonetheless Pakistan desperately needed more tanks to defend itself against India in the future and with Chinese assistance set up a tank rebuild factory at Taxila in the late 1970s. This was equipped to overhaul tank engines as well as repair and manufacture parts needed for the rebuild programme. Colonel Borisov may have had political motives for criticizing the Type 59, but China's willingness to open the Taxila plant not only signalled Pakistan's commitment to the tank but also that there was an underlying problem with it.

By the mid-1990s Pakistan had massed a mighty tank fleet some 2,000 strong, that included 1,200 Type 59s, 200 Type 69s and around 50 T-54/55s. Even in 2005 it was assessed to be still operating 1,100 Type 59s and 400 Type 69s. The Bangladeshi Army created after the war was equipped with T-54/55 and Type 59/69 tanks.

Hispanic Tanks

The T-54/55 even got as far as Latin America and the Caribbean. In particular Cuba ended up with a vast tank fleet. Thanks to America's Cold War stand-off with Castro's regime, Moscow supplied the Cubans with a vast array of weapons. Even before the 1962 missile crisis Castro had taken receipt of up to 50 T-54s as well as 100 T-34s. In the mid-1980s he had 350 T-54/55s. By the early 1990s the Cuban Army had amassed in the region of 1,200. Quite what Castro intended to do with them in the confines of Cuba is unclear and most ended up unused in storage.

In Central America in the mid-1980s to help Nicaragua's Marxist Sandinista government, against the American-backed Contras, they received Soviet weapons including twenty T-55s. By the early 1990s the Sandinistas had about 130, but they had little value in the counter-insurgency war. The only South American country to purchase large amounts of Soviet military equipment was Peru, which ended up with 300 T-54/55s.

Opposite: Somali T-55 captured by the Ethiopians in 1978 during the Ogaden War – it appears to bear the turret number '010'.

T-55s on parade with the Ugandan Army in Kampala in 1976. They feature a very distinctive camouflage that would have helped conceal them fighting in the African bush.

Flipped Ethiopian T-54/55 that seems to have slid off the escarpment to the left.

This tank was identified as a T-55 belonging to the Somali National Army, but a ventilator dome is clearly visible on top of the turret. Ethiopia, Somalia and neighbouring Yemen all took receipt of deliveries of T-54/55s.

Lurking in the bush, a government T-55 during the Angolan Civil War.

Angolan Army T-54/55s captured by UNITA were used to defend their strongholds at Jamba and Mavinga.

This Libyan Army T-55 was built in Poland and abandoned in 2011 during the uprising that toppled Colonel Gaddafi.

Indian T-54 fitted with a dummy fume extractor making it appear that the 100mm is a 105mm gun. This was done during the 1971 Indo-Pakistan War for recognition purposes as both sides used the T-54/55.

Tank park in Afghanistan containing at least nine T-54/55s and a ARV. The Afghan National Army, Soviet Army, Mujahedeen, Taliban and many other warring factions made use of this tank.

A Northern Alliance T-54 in Afghanistan greeted by wary villagers.

Chapter Nine

Desert Failure

The T-54/55 fought with all the Arab states during the Arab-Israeli Wars of 1967, 1973 and 1982 except for Jordan. The Israelis captured so many that they redeployed them, as well as supplying them to their South Lebanese allies. It was also extensively used during the bitter Iran-Iraq War of 1980–8.

Middle Eastern Conflict

Many Arab countries in the Middle East were initially equipped with British and American surplus Second World War armaments. During the 1950s, however, the Soviet Union stepped into the breach. Egypt was one of the very first recipients of the T-54/55 from the Soviet Union with 120 delivered in 1956 following the Suez Crisis. These were used to re-equip the Egyptian forces routed in the Sinai campaign. In the early 1960s another 270 were supplied by Moscow.

The Soviet Union sent instructors but their training was unimaginative. Crews were taught little more than basic driving and gunnery. To ensure the shock of a massed attack, tank crews were instructed to stick together – showing initiative was not required. The Egyptians used their T-54/55s to equip three units protecting Sinai, consisting of the 4th and 7th Armoured Divisions and the 6th Mechanized Division.

In the battles fought in Sinai during the 1967 Six Day War General Arik (Ariel) Sharon's Israeli armoured division initially came up against elderly T-34/85s supporting the Egyptian infantry divisions. Unfortunately Lieutenant Colonel Natke Nir, leading Sharon's Centurion tank battalion, had his command vehicle taken out by a T-54 as the radio operator witnessed first-hand:

> It was at five in the morning. We noticed the entrenched Egyptian force only when they opened fire. We tried to move away looking for shelter but it was too late and our half-track was hit by a T-54 tank's gun. I was operating the machine gun and I saw Natke being hit. I tried to help him, not realizing my own wound, but when I attempted to stand up there were no legs to stand on and I collapsed.

The tanks of the Egyptian 4th Armoured Division were mauled at Bir Lahfan and Bir Gifgafah. Although they avoided being completely trapped by the Israelis, only about 30 per cent of the division managed to withdraw over the Suez Canal. The Egyptians were outfought and abandoned their T-34/85s and T-54/55s wholesale. After some 370 T-54/55s were lost in Sinai, the Soviets moved swiftly to replace them. By 1969 another 800 had been shipped to Egypt from the Soviet Union. Syria likewise was supplied 150 Soviet-built T-54s in the late 1950s followed by a similar number after the Six Day War.

Despite the lacklustre performance of T-54/55 units both in Sinai and on the Golan Heights, by the time of the 1973 Yom Kippur War the tank formed the backbone of both Egypt and Syria's powerful tank fleets. The Egyptians attacked the Israelis using their 4th and 21st Armoured Divisions and the 6th and 23rd Mechanized Divisions. They also had the 3rd Mechanized Division in reserve. The key forces committed to the offensive on the Golan comprised the Syrian 1st and 3rd Armoured Divisions supported by the Iraqi 3rd Armoured Division. All these formations were largely equipped with T-54/55s. Once again, though, superior Israeli training and gunnery prevailed. The Israelis also used a few of their captured T-54/55s in 1973, deploying them to the Sinai with the 11th (Reserve) Armoured Brigade.

The fighting in the Yom Kippur conflict was confused, with the fog of war contributing to some bizarre incidents notably on the Syrian front. In one, a lost Syrian T-55 blundered right into the middle of some Israeli half-tracks belonging to a headquarters company. Major Itzik, their operations officer, takes up the story:

> Most uncomfortable. Nobody knew quite what to do. It was clearly unwise to provoke the tank, which could have obliterated them all, so none of the Israelis fired. Fortunately, the Syrian crew were as puzzled: the T-55 wheeled round and left without firing a shot.

At Kuneitra the Israeli Air Force reaped a bloody harvest. *The Sunday Times*, reporting on the fighting, observed the carnage first-hand:

> Israeli air strikes caught the retreating Syrian column on the road back home about two miles north-east of Kuneitra. The road was cluttered with the ruins of their tanks. Two men from one T-54 had tried to run for it when the planes swooped down: their corpses lay as they had been hit, both staring back over their shoulders. Besides another tank, the driver lay beneath a blanket as if asleep, his head on a pillow. Perhaps he had been exhausted and trying to snatch a fifteen minute doze? His face was quite relaxed: he must have died in his sleep as the Israeli fighters' cannon blew off both his legs.

Many of the surviving Middle-Eastern T-54/55s and subsequent replacements remained in service: by the late 1970s Egypt still possessed around 850 and Syria had 1,500. Gaddafi's Libya and Saddam's Iraq had similar numbers to Syria. Many, though, were believed to be in storage, cannibalized for spares or were sold off over the years.

The Iraqis received their first Soviet T-54s in 1959 when they were supplied eighty of them. During the 1960s they received another batch of seventy. Around fifty refurbished T-54 were also despatched to troubled Yemen in 1968. By the time Saddam Hussein attacked neighbouring Iran in 1980 he had in the region of 2,500 T-54/55s and T-62s. However, the eight-year war was not characterized by armoured warfare and rapidly bogged down into a senseless bloody conflict of attrition.

The Eastern Bloc was swift to make good Saddam's initial combat losses. In early 1981 East Germany or Poland supplied 100 T-55s via Saudi Arabia. Three years later in May 1984 Saddam signed a very large weapons deal with Moscow that included some 200 T-55s. China was likewise quick to capitalise on the Iran-Iraq War. It exported up to 2,500 Type 59s and Type 69s in 1982–9, many of which went to Iraq and Iran. The Chinese signed a contract in 1981 with Saddam to supply 500–600 Type 59s. The year after this was followed by another deal for 400 Type 69s. All deliveries were completed by 1986. Initially Iraq ordered up to 200 Type 69-Is, armed with the smoothbore 100mm gun, which were delivered via Saudi Arabia in 1983. These were followed by Type 69-IIs. Iran also obtained about 400 Type 59/69s.

After the Iran-Iraq War, Saddam's T-55s and Type 69s were involved in the 1991 Gulf War and the 2003 Iraq War. They were now easily outclassed by the T-72 that equipped his Republican Guard. By this stage both were obsolete when they came up against the British Challenger and the American Abrams.

At the time of the Syrian uprising in 2011 President Assad's military was assessed to still have as many as 2,000 T-55s. However, the bulk of these were in storage as the Syrian Army's main tank force comprised 2,600 T-72s and T-62s and it was these that bore the brunt of the fighting.

Desert Shortcomings

The T-54 was developed drawing on Soviet experience gained in Europe during the Second World War. What was needed was a tank that could be used for a shock massed attack, that would simply overwhelm an enemy and then exploit a breakthrough. If the Cold War had turned hot, the T-54's low profile would have been ideal on the open North German Plain, but this low turret reduced main armament depression to just five degrees. In contrast, Western tanks could manage 10 degrees; furthermore, the larger fighting compartment in Western tanks ensured greater crew comfort and just as important a faster rate of fire.

The T-54/55 was never really intended to fight in the heat of the Middle East and it was there that its shortcomings became most apparent. The cramped fighting compartment became unbearably stifling in the desert, forcing Arab crews to drive round with their engine louvres vulnerably open. The baking heat inevitably reduced crew efficiency, not least the accuracy of their gunnery. Choking dust also reduced visibility forcing tank commanders to fight with their head exposed. This was not a drawback for Israeli tank commanders, who preferred to fight that way.

The British-supplied Centurion and American M48/60 Patton armed with a 105mm outgunned the T-54. In 1967 the Israelis' Centurions had better ammunition and an effective killing range of 2,000m, the T-54 managing only 1,000m. The latter was hampered by the primitive quality of its anti-tank ammunition. This was basic armour-piercing, a solid, full-calibre shot made of steel that offered limited penetration at long range. Due to energy dissipation, the shot only had 50 per cent armour penetration compared to other more modern types of round. Although the armour-piercing shell of the T-54/55 could cut through armour twice as thick as its own diameter, this was only achievable at close range. Therefore the shot's 100mm could penetrate 200m of armour, but the trick was to get close enough without being destroyed in the process. At maximum range the T-54/55 rounds tended to glance off the angles of the Centurion's armour.

The Soviets' later T-62 MBT fired a more sophisticated armour-piercing fin stabilized discarding sabot (APFSDS) round that was tipped with a dart or arrow, which concentrated the striking energy in one spot. This type of tank, though, was never available to the Arabs in great numbers. Israeli tanks fired the similar armour-piercing discarding sabot as well as high explosive anti-tank that forced molten metal into its target. Both had distinctive narrow tips like the APFSDS, designed to cut through hardened tank armour and remained very lethal at longer ranges.

Some T-55s were fitted with infra-red searchlights which gave the Arabs a decided advantage in night combat with the Israelis. Historian Max Hastings, who covered the Yom Kippur battles as a war correspondent wrote:

> Very fortunately for the Israelis, the Syrians neither exploited their Soviet night-vision equipment effectively, nor used smoke to cover their own advance, which could have been fatal for the defenders, who relied overwhelmingly on the eyes of their gunners to destroy the Arab tank columns.

The T-54/55 did offer the Arab armies some other advantages. Its low profile made it a smaller target compared to the Israeli tanks. In addition its weight meant it could cross ground that the heavier and slower Centurions and Pattons could not.

However, geography also greatly hampered the T-54/55; in flat desert, dunes and the Golan Heights it proved to be vulnerable.

During the Arab-Israeli Wars tank commanders liked to fight from a 'hull-down' position, i.e. dug in or from behind a sand dune, which only exposed part of the turret. The T-54/55's limited depression meant that the tank had to be driven up the rise it was sheltering behind to engage enemy tanks coming down the opposite slopes. This gave the Israelis a notable advantage when the Arab tanks exposed themselves. Iraq's T-54/55 and Type 69 faced exactly the same problems.

Nonetheless, the performance of the T-54/55 should not be too undervalued. In 1973, in combination with other Soviet weapon systems, it came very, very close to overwhelming the state of Israel. It was poor leadership and training, particularly on the Egyptian side, that enabled the Israelis after suffering heavy losses to eventually turn the tide.

The Israelis came up against their old adversary again in 1982 when they drove the Palestinian Liberation Organization (PLO) from Beirut. The PLO had about twenty T-54/55s and sixty T-34/85s. The Israelis dealt with them easily. Israel's allies, consisting of Christian Lebanese militias led by the South Lebanese Army, also had about sixty T-54s and elderly Shermans. Both had been supplied by the Israelis.

During the invasion of southern Lebanon, the Israeli armour clashed with the Syrians in the Beka'a Valley. Their main tank force comprised the T-62 and T-72, but they still had 1,500 T-54/55s in reserve. Some of these saw action, as journalist John Laffin recalled:

> On 14 June [1982] the Syrian 85th Mechanized Brigade, with T-55 tanks and BTR-60 and BMP APCs, attacked Israeli armour south-east of Beirut and closed to within 100 and even 50 metres. They fought so stubbornly that they lost all their tanks and other vehicles. This did not say much for their leadership, but proved the ability of Syrian troops to stand up to pitched battle.

According to Israeli sources, the Syrian Army lost 334 tanks including 125 T-54/55s.

Knocked-out Egyptian T-54. It is painted in a very pale sand colour, and on the left-hand side of the turret is the traditional Egyptian red and green turret flash. The front external fuel tank has exploded.

More knocked-out Egyptian T-54s lost in Sinai.

Egyptian T-54 (turret number 421) on guard duty. Note the dust cover on the barrel. It has a two-tone camouflage scheme of sand and light brown.

Dug-in Iraqi T-55s photographed during the Iran-Iraq War.

Burnt-out Iraqi T-54A or Type 59, a victim of Operation Desert Storm in 1991.

Another Iraqi T-54/55 or Type 59/69 blown apart during Desert Storm. The blast has torn the turret off and blown the engine out of the hull.

Hull-down Iraqi T-55 lost during the retreat from Kuwait.

Iraqi Type 59/69 amidst Kuwait's burning oilfields in 1991.

Famous shot of an abandoned Iraqi T-54/55 on the outskirts of Kuwait City in 1991. It had a sand base colour with patches of dark green.

Completely burnt-out T-55 belonging to the Iraqi Army destroyed in 2003. The glacis plate has been pierced.

Crude uparmouring using track shoes wedged in the turret handrails.

The main gun barrel and fume extractor of a T-54/55 frames Kuwait's blazing oil wells in 1991.

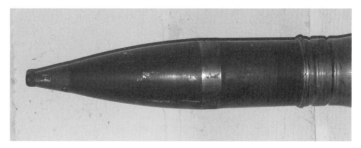

The solid steel shot had limited penetration at long ranges and this led to the development of the 9K116 Bastion system that enabled the 100mm gun to fire the AT-10 'Stabber' laser-guided projectile.

During the Middle Eastern wars the T-54/55 was hampered by the ineffectiveness of its armoured-piercing ammunition which dissipated much of its kinetic energy.

Chapter Ten

European Swansong

After the death of Mao Zedong, the Chinese PLA struggled to modernize, having previously been an almost entirely infantry force. In the Korean War the PLA suffered the most appalling losses and it was obvious that it needed armoured support. This experience had driven the development of their Type 59 MBT.

China's subsequent views on modern armoured warfare were mainly shaped by studying the Middle Eastern conflicts. Despite the Arab-Israeli wars, by the late 1970s China only had a dozen armoured divisions, scarcely enough to protect its vast frontiers. The Chinese, though, were happy to supply their allies and client states with hundreds of tanks.

Southeast Asian Wars

The North Vietnamese did not deploy their T-54s until late in the Vietnam War, although deliveries of T-54A, T-54B and Type 59 tanks began in the 1960s. They also obtained some 200 Type 62 light tanks, but these were difficult to tell apart from the Type 59 and 150 Type 63 light amphibious tanks. Their tanks first went into combat in neighbouring Laos in early 1971 when seven were lost resisting South Vietnamese tanks near Hill 31.

The North's 1972 Easter Offensive, launched from North Vietnam, Laos and Cambodia, was fought as a conventional battle and its tank crews, lacking infantry and artillery support, suffered at the hands of the better-trained South Vietnamese. Three years later when the North marched to victory it had 600 T-54s and Type 59s spearheading the final attack on Saigon. Three decades later Vietnam still has 850 T-54/55s and 350 Type 59s.

The defining moment of the Vietnam War came on 30 April 1975 when the North's Soviet-built T-54s surrounded the Presidential Palace in Saigon. A tank bearing the turret number '844' symbolically crashed through the gates. South Vietnamese officers at the palace then surrendered under the watchful eye of a North Vietnamese Type 63. It was one of the high points in the T-54's career and an iconic episode in the wider Cold War. It was also a humiliating moment for American foreign policy in Southeast Asia.

Ironically, several hundred Chinese tanks, including Type 59s, were involved in China's invasion of northern Vietnam in 1979 in response to Vietnamese actions in Cambodia. This region was not suitable for tank warfare and tough Vietnamese resistance persuaded the Chinese to withdraw after they suffered an estimated 26,000 dead and 37,000 wounded. Notably, the Chinese lost tanks at Cao Bang. The Vietnamese claimed rather fancifully to have destroyed 280 tanks during the fighting, which is probably more than were committed to the invasion.

Even if exaggerated, Chinese casualties and the swift end to the war highlighted the shortcomings of the PLA. Although the Type 59 upgrade was underway in the shape of the Type 69, it was not available in 1979. When the latter first appeared military experts considered it a formidable weapon, bearing little resemblance to the obsolete T-54 from which it was derived. Nonetheless, it was a prime example of China's continued policy of modernizing its armed forces by improving old, obsolete Soviet designs and utilizing existing factories rather than importing new weapons.

Thailand placed an order from some 500 Type 69-IIs in the late 1980s. The intention was to use this impressive tank fleet to equip an armoured division, a cavalry division and the tank battalions assigned to four reserve infantry divisions. By the mid-1990s, however, reports indicated that only 50 to 150 tanks had been delivered. This deal seems to have been abandoned because a decade later Thailand had just fifty Type 69s and these were in storage.

Modernize or Retire

At the height of the Cold War in the late 1970s most Warsaw Pact countries still had thousands of T-54/55s available. For example, Bulgaria had 1,800, East Germany 2,500, Hungary 1,000, Poland 3,800 and Romania 1,500. Many of these were retained even after the collapse of the Soviet Union and the Warsaw Pact.

By the 1970s and 1980s the D-10T 100mm gun was woefully inadequate against modern Western tanks. The AP and HVAPDS-T ammunition for the D-10T lacked penetration power sufficient to kill the latest generation of NATO armour except at very close range. Even the introduction of the 9K116 Bastion anti-tank guided missile in the early 1980s had limited effectiveness against Western tanks employing Chobham-style armour. Nevertheless, the T-55 continued to see action during the 1990s with the breakup of the Soviet Union and Yugoslavia.

The end of the Cold War inevitably meant that thousands of surplus-to-requirements T-54/55s came onto the market. After the fall of the Soviet Union, the Russian Federation alone still had about 4,000 and Ukraine almost 700. Both countries subsequently offered upgrade packages. For some armies it seemed modernizing their T-54/55 tank fleets was a much cheaper option than purchasing replacement tanks. In the 1980s Czechoslovakia, Poland and East Germany upgraded their T-55s to the AM2 standard. Finland went down this route with its T-55M modernization. After the division of Czechoslovakia the Czech Republic offered its T-55AM2 package for export, but there was little interest.

Even Romania, with its troubled tank programme, offered an upgrade for existing T-54As. Some of this undoubtedly drew on its indigenous TR-85 and TR-580 tanks. The modification was quite extensive, offering a thermal sleeve for the 100mm gun, smoke grenade launcher system, a new anti-aircraft machine-gun mount, new engine, new fire-control system, infra-red headlamp, L-2G infra-red weapon sight assembly and anti-radiation and napalm shielding. These improvements were installed in some Romanian and Iraqi tanks.

Many Western defence companies, seeing what they thought was a golden opportunity, also offered upgrade packages. These though often proved simply too expensive for countries trying to cut back their defence budgets at the end of the Cold War. Few could be enticed when the cost was more than the original value of the tank. Egypt, with 1,000 T-54/55s, seemed potentially a prime customer and was courted by many Western firms.

Ambitious Egyptian plans included the American Ramses II programme as well as the German Jung Jungenthal upgrade but neither got beyond the prototype stage during the 1980s. Once the Egyptians had been gifted American M60 tanks and began building the American M1A1 Abrams in the 1990s, such requirements swiftly fell by the wayside. Almost two decades later, despite being superfluous, the Ramses II armed with a 105mm gun finally appeared in 2005 with several hundred tanks upgraded. After 60 years of continuous service the T-54/55 continues to soldier on in various parts of the world.

European Swansong

Following Moscow's military interventions in Hungary and Czechoslovakia, the T-54/55 did not see any further action in Europe until after the Cold War. It was involved in extensive fighting during the violent decade-long breakup of Yugoslavia in the 1990s. At the start of the various wars of succession, the *Jugoslovenska Narodna Armija* (JNA – Yugoslav National Army) tank holdings included around 750 T-54/55s. From photographic evidence, most of these appear to have been T-55s as they lacked the ventilator dome. Although obsolete by modern standards, the T-54/55 provided valuable direct artillery support to the various warring factions.

The first T-55s to be lost were a dozen captured by the Slovenes at the Sentilij border post near Austria on 29 June 1991. These were quickly reorganized as the Slovene 7th District Tank Company and turned against the JNA during the brief Ten

Day War. In September 1991, in what was dubbed the 'Barracks War', the Croats seized JNA T-55s at Sibenik. More rugged than the M-84 (the Yugoslav copy of the Soviet T-72), the T-55 played an important role in the battles fought between the Croats and Serbs.

In a show of force, JNA T-55s were sent to the plains of Slavonia in the autumn of 1991 as part of a general offensive against newly-independent Croatia. During the bitter fighting for the city of Novska, the Croatian defenders did not succumb to the Serbians' superior firepower, instead stopping JNA T-55s in the streets using hand-held anti-tank weapons. A foreign volunteer recalled 'Only the rear of the tank is vulnerable to light rocket launchers. But it's a dangerous game, and inevitably, we always lost one or two men in such attacks.' On one occasion at Novska, a T-55 serving with a Serbian militia trying to escape trouble reversed into a deep concrete storm drain and became stranded with its hull and gun almost vertical. Caught in no man's land neither side were able to retrieve it until the fighting ended.

At Vukovar the Croatian defenders counter-attacked with T-55s retrieved from ex-Federal barracks but any gains were soon lost to the superior JNA forces. On the Dalmatian coast, the town of Zadar was one of the Serbs' major objectives, but the Croatian Tiger Brigade, supported by T-55s, thwarted them. This unit was issued with the best equipment available to the Croatian Army and deployed as a fire brigade all over Croatia. After being used in a conventional role in the short autumn campaign, the tanks of both sides dug in and became static artillery. Later in Bosnia-Herzegovina Serbian T-55s were able to shell Sarajevo with impunity.

British mercenaries serving with the Croatian National Guard fought JNA T-55s at Osijek and Velika Pumpa. Sometimes the Serb tank forces were not as formidable as they first appeared. In one instant at Osijek of a grouping of twenty-five JNA T-55s and a single T-72, it transpired only twelve were actual tanks, the rest being wooden dummies. At Velika Pumpa the Croats and their allies had to rely on rocket-propelled grenades and one-shot rocket launchers to fend off a force of seven T-55s and a T-72. They claimed to have knocked out four of the T-55s and the T-72.

In the spring of 1992 a force of thirty Croatian T-55s rolled into western Bosnia to secure lines of communication with the Bosnian Croats, resulting in fighting near Kupres. The 1st Guards Brigade of the Bosnian Croat Army was equipped with T-55s.

Tanks fighting in built-up areas were at risk not only from anti-tank teams but also from unarmed civilians, including women and children. Lieutenant Nick Richardson, RN, whose Harrier was shot down near Gorazde in 1994 trying to protect the town from Serb T-55s, witnessed this. After being rescued, he joined an SAS team in the town and was taken up onto a rooftop to see a destroyed tank 2km to the north-west:

It turned out that the tank, a T-55 like the pair I'd tried to bomb on the ridgeline, had been jumped on by hundreds of civilians when it had made an attempt to break through the defences and carve a pathway into town. After it had crushed a few townspeople under its tracks, the Muslims got their revenge. They dragged out the crew, chopped them into pieces, then threw the bits back into the tank and set fire to it.

In response to NATO fighter-bombers, the Serbs became adept at concealing their tanks. NATO used it airpower in 1999 to drive the JNA from Kosovo claiming ninety-three tanks destroyed in air strikes. Investigators subsequently confirmed only fourteen tanks destroyed, most of which were T-55s.

While the Croatian Homeland War ended in 1995, the fighting in other republics of former Yugoslavia did not end until 2001. By that staged Croatia had amassed 220 T-55s and Serbia maintained a force of over 700, while in contrast Bosnia and Slovenia had fewer than 100 each. It seemed that despite being retired in the rest of Europe the T-54/55's European swansong was potentially not quite over.

Chinese-built Type 59 captured by South Vietnamese troops on 4 July 1972 and preserved in the Australian Armoured Corps Museum.

South Vietnamese soldiers from the 20th Tank Regiment with a damaged North Vietnamese Type 59 captured in 1972 south of Dong Ha during the North's Easter Offensive.

North Vietnamese T-54 on the streets of Saigon in 1975 marking the end of the Vietnam War.

T-54Bs serving with the Cambodian Army at the end of the Cambodian Civil War.

Chinese tank destroyed at Cao Bang during the invasion of Vietnam in 1979. The length of the barrel suggests it was a Type 62 light tank.

Four JNA T-55s ambushed by Slovenian forces on the Italian border at Rožna Dolina in the suburbs of Nova Gorica in western Slovenia in 1991. They all have unusual large stowage boxes on the right-hand side of their turrets. These were not typical of other JNA tanks.

Burning T-55 lost in the fighting between the Croats and Serbians for Vukovar in 1991. The Croatian defenders had a number of ex-JNA tanks.

Destroyed Serbian T-55 in Bosnia in 1997.

T-55s belonging to Bosnian-Croat forces on exercise in 1998. They have a three-tone camouflage scheme of pale green, brown and dark green (or black).

Serbian inspectors examining armoured vehicles including a T-55 belonging to the Croatian 3rd Mechanized Brigade at Đakovo in 2003.

The T-54/55 has a remarkable track record that will never be surpassed.

Chapter Eleven

How to Win Friends

In light of the T-54/55 being produced in China, Czechoslovakia, Pakistan, Poland, Ukraine, Romania and Russia, it was a truly an international tank. In contrast, outside the Soviet Union the T-34 was only built by the Czechs and the Poles, though there is some evidence that China reverse-engineered it and produced limited numbers. Both the T-34/85 and T-54/55 were brothers in arms and were involved in many of the same wars, with both seeing action during the breakup of Yugoslavia in the 1990s.

What possessed Moscow to let the Non-Soviet Warsaw Pact members build the T-54/55? Especially as there was always a very real danger they could be turned against the Soviet Army. Fortunately for Moscow, in 1968 Czech T-54/55s did not resist the overwhelming Warsaw Pact invasion. In 1981 in the face of Solidarity's growing agitation for democracy, the Polish Army declared martial law and put its T-55 tanks onto the streets, thereby narrowly pre-empting Warsaw Pact intervention.

There were a number of factors for this willingness to share. Firstly, Moscow needed its East European allies to build up their armoured forces during the 1950s and 1960s to support Soviet forces as quickly as possible. Secondly, when they exported tanks it gave the Soviet Union plausible deniability, even though everyone knew the hand of Moscow was behind them. When Czechoslovakia, East Germany and Poland shipped tanks to the Middle East, Moscow argued it had no influence over such matters. China of course was a completely different case – it had its own agenda in the Indian Sub-continent, Middle East and Southeast Asia when it came to tank sales.

China recognized the utility of the T-54 from the very start and simply copied it. What is not entirely clear is whether initial Soviet deliveries were with a view to supplying more tanks or assisting the Chinese to build their own. Once Sino-Soviet relations deteriorated it is unlikely that Beijing had permission to produce its own version. What is interesting is that despite capturing the Soviet Union's newer T-62 during the Sino-Soviet border clashes, instead of copying it the Chinese cherry picked some of the better features and incorporated them in their Type 69, which essentially remained a copy of the T-54. The Chinese brazenly called it the Type 69 because it was in March 1969 that they captured a T-62 on the Ussuri River following fighting with the Soviets.

The Chinese occupied Damansky Island which they called Zhenbao. Their troops ambushed a Soviet patrol sparking more fighting involving artillery and tanks. The Soviets committed four T-62s to the island and promptly had one disabled by Chinese artillery fire. Soviet attempts to recover or destroy it failed and the Chinese hauled the tank to their side of the river. At the time it was a welcome intelligence windfall and a sobering setback for the Soviet Army. Moscow got revenge in August 1969 when it attacked on the Kazakhstan-Xinjiang border thousands of miles to the north-west. Soviet armour pushed deep into China, surrounding and destroying a Chinese force.

These incidents not only contributed to the development of the Type 69 but also had a significant impact on the stance of the Chinese armed forces. Beijing accused Moscow of stationing about 65 divisions with 15,000 tanks supported by several thousand aircraft along the border. Very slowly, so as not to antagonise the Soviet Union into outright war, Chairman Mao deployed almost all his armoured units and 50 per cent of the entire PLA to face China's northern borders.

Mao had no real defence against the Soviet Union's tens of thousands of T-54/55 and T-62 tanks. In light of how easily the Soviets had swept through Manchuria and defeated the occupying Japanese in 1945, Mao was alarmed at the prospect of the Soviet Army striking toward Beijing. Soviet paratroops had landed as far west as Baotou in 1945 and they had temporarily occupied an area bigger than Eastern Europe. In the 1960s Mao's response was to build enormous tank obstacles up to 40m high, 400m wide and 220m deep. They were widely viewed as a complete waste of time and the project was eventually abandoned.

After Mao's death the PLA had around a dozen armoured divisions with at most 9,000 tanks: in stark contrast the Soviet Army had around 50 tank divisions equipped with some 50,000 tanks, the bulk of which were MBTs. Mao's fears were well founded: the PLA relied on manpower, and had Moscow deployed even half its tank force against China it would have been overwhelmed

The hugely successful T-54/55 was built or assembled in at least a dozen factories, including Nizhnyi Tagil in Russia, Omsk in Russia, the Malyshev plant in Kharkov in Ukraine, ZTS Martin in Czechoslovakia, Bumar-Labedy in Poland, Bucharest/Braşov in Romania, Baotou, Beijing, Changchun and Harbin in China and Taxila in Pakistan. Combined, they produced in the region of 80,000 to 100,000 tanks. It is impossible to be precise, as the Soviets and Chinese never issued official production figures. In the late 1970s the US Department of Defense estimated that the Soviet Union was building 3,000 tanks a year with another 800 produced by the Non-Soviet Warsaw Pact countries. This output included the T-62 and T-72.

The secret behind the T-54/55's incredible success, like the T-34/85, was its simplicity. It was relatively easy and cheap to build, unlike its increasingly complex and costly successors. Outside the Soviet Union the T-62 was only built by Czechoslovakia for export, while the T-64 was only ever produced in the Soviet Union and never exported. The subsequent T-72 and T-80 were built by a number of foreign manufacturers, but never in the same quantities as the T-54/55.

An array of Soviet T-55s on manoeuvres. Only the lead tank and the second from the left are fitted with laser rangefinders over the 100mm gun, which greatly increased its effective range. Note the absence of the loader's cupola with its anti-aircraft machine gun.

This is the Soviet T-62 captured during the brief 1969 Sino-Soviet border war, displayed in Beijing's military museum. This was used to help improve the Chinese Type 59 and resulted in the Type 69, though they did not adopt the larger 115mm gun.

Romanian TR-85 on the streets during the 1989 uprising against Nicolae Ceauşescu.

The same but not. Two Iraqi T-55s on the Basra-Kuwait Highway during the Gulf War. The one to the right is a Soviet Model 1970 with the anti-aircraft gun mount over the loader's hatch, while the one to the left is of Polish origin as it has the different-style gunner's aperture. The glacis marking on the second tank is a unit vehicle registration.

Derelict Iraqi T-54 on the highway outside Kuwait City.

Burning remains of an Iraqi Type 69. Iraq's Chinese tanks did not fare well in the Gulf and Iraq Wars as they were outclassed.

Burned-out Iraqi T-55 on the outskirts of Kuwait City. The rubber tyres on the road wheels have melted in the heat of the fire.

Iraqi Type 69 ablaze on Highway 27 in April 2003 during Operation Iraqi Freedom.

More Middle Eastern debris of war. Iraqi T-54/55s destroyed on the road to Basra in 2003.

Early-model T-54 in Afghanistan with counterweight on the barrel.

More abandoned Afghan T-54s. This was the fate of thousands of T-54/55s after the Cold War.

Iraqi T-55 dubbed 'Soviet made shit' – it in fact came from Poland.

Postscript:
'Soviet made shit'

On the highway outside Kuwait city just after the Gulf War ended some joker sprayed 'Soviet made shit' on the upper glacis plate of an abandoned Iraqi T-55. It was an act of triumphant bravado. By this stage in the tank's 45-year history this comment was a little harsh but essentially true.

The initial T-54/55 design appeared in the late 1940s, but had long since been obsolete once it was no longer an adequate tank-to-tank weapon. The 1960s had been its heyday. Yet whenever it was called upon to fight where there were no next generation tanks it remained a valuable instrument of war on the battlefield. This was particularly so during the numerous 'bush wars' and regional conflicts fought during the Cold War and indeed the Balkan Wars. By 1991 though it was definitely no longer a front-line tank and Saddam Hussein's generals knew that but they had little choice but employ it.

Ironically, this particular T-55 singled out by the eloquent graffiti artist had not been built in the Soviet Union, rather in Poland, the more oval cover over the gunner's telescope aperture on the turret indicating this. Coalition troops understandably had little time for such subtle nuances, and anyway it was designed in the Soviet Union. Imagine if this was one of the Polish tanks delivered in the early 1980s. Having survived the destruction of the Iran-Iraq War, it finally came a cropper in the battle for Kuwait.

The humiliating defeat of Saddam Hussein's army in 1991 was an embarrassment to Moscow and came as a shock to all the Soviet client states. It clearly showed that armies equipped with Soviet-era armour could not stand up to modern Western armies. In the last two major wars that involved the T-54/55, many of than were not actually Soviet-built but foreign pretenders to the throne. During the Gulf War and Iraq War many of the Iraqi T-54/55s encountered were Chinese-built Type 69s and Polish T-55s. They say imitation is the greatest form of flattery.

Like its predecessor the T-34, when Soviet tank designers came up with the T-54/55 they produced an even more durable and long-lasting tank. The T-54/55 became omnipresent during the Cold War, making it the most ubiquitous tank in history. It has since, like the Kalashnikov assault rifle, become one of the great icons of the Cold War.

Further Reading

Tucker-Jones, Anthony, *Soviet Cold War Weaponry: Tanks and Armoured Vehicles*
(Pen & Sword Military, 2015)

Tucker-Jones, Anthony, *T-34: The Red Army's Legendary Medium Tank*
(Pen & Sword Military, 2015)

Tucker-Jones, Anthony, *The Iraq War: Operation Iraqi Freedom 2003-2011*
(Pen & Sword Military, 2014)

Tucker-Jones, Anthony, *The Gulf War: Operation Desert Storm 1990-1991*
(Pen & Sword Military, 2014)

Tucker-Jones, Anthony, *Armoured Warfare in the Arab-Israeli Conflicts*
(Pen & Sword Military, 2013)

Tucker-Jones, Anthony, *The Soviet-Afghan War* (Pen & Sword Military, 2012)